Lynda Field is a trained counsellor and psychotherapist who specialises in personal and group development. She is the author of many best-selling titles, including *Weekend Life Coach*, *60 Ways to Feel Amazing* and *60 Ways to Change Your Life*. In addition to giving seminars and workshops worldwide, she runs a telephone and online coaching service, and writes articles for a variety of national magazines. She lives in Essex, UK.

Visit Lynda online at www.weekendlifecoach.com or email her at lyndafield@weekendlifecoach.com

How to kick the self-doubt habit in 48 hours

Lynda Field

Vermilion
LONDON

1 3 5 7 9 10 8 6 4 2

Reissued in 2007.

First published in 2006 by Vermilion,
an imprint of Ebury Publishing, Random House,
20 Vauxhall Bridge Road, London SW1V 2SA

Random House Australia (Pty) Limited
20 Alfred Street, Milsons Point, Sydney,
New South Wales 2061, Australia

Random House New Zealand Limited
18 Poland Road, Glenfield,
Auckland 10, New Zealand

Random House South Africa (Pty) Limited
Isle of Houghton, Corner Boundary Road & Carse O'Gowrie,
Houghton 2198, South Africa

Random House Publishers India Private Limited
301 World Trade Tower, Hotel Intercontinental Grand Complex,
Barakhamba Lane, New Delhi 110 001 India

The Random House Group Limited Reg. No. 954009

Papers used by Vermilion are natural, recyclable products
made from wood grown in sustainable forests.

Typeset by SX Composing DTP, Rayleigh, Essex
Printed and bound in Great Britain by
Mackays of Chatham plc, Chatham, Kent

A CIP catalogue record for this book is available from
the British Library

ISBN 978-0-0919-0687-0

Contents

*This book is dedicated to the memory of
my fabulous mother-in-law Mary Field.
You taught me the greatest lesson and
you are in my heart, always.*

Acknowledgements

THANK YOU TO:

My husband, Richard, who is the love of my life.

My children, Leilah, Jack and Alex, who are my pride and joy.

Alaska, my granddaughter, who is full of fun and love.

My parents, Barbara and Idwal Goronwy, who taught me all I know.

The rest of my fabulous family whose love and support make everything possible.

Barbara Higham, who is always there for me.

Sue Roberts, a treasured confidante.

Phraid Gower, my oldest friend from schooldays.

All my clients and colleagues who keep me on my toes and remind me of what is important.

The wonderful team at Ebury who have supported me all the way. With extra special thanks to my brilliant editor Judith Kendra, who is always full of new ideas and ready to take a chance, and also to Caroline Newbury for her diligence, creativity and eternal optimism. This book is the result of a real team effort!

Preface

That Magic Sparkle of Confidence

People are like stained-glass windows. They sparkle and shine when the sun is out, but when the darkness sets in their true beauty is revealed only if there is light from within.

ELISABETH KÜBLER-ROSS

It's so easy to feel good about ourselves when things are going well, isn't it? We feel more positive and attractive and our expectations rise as we slip effortlessly into the cycle of success, where our upbeat energy attracts more of the same and our positive expectations are fulfilled. In other words when we are feeling great it shows; others respond to our powerful personal magnetism and the doors of opportunity open up before us! Don't you just love this feeling, when everything feels 'right' and you flowing along and life is sweet?

You will definitely know if you are experiencing this cycle right now, the key indicators are: high self-esteem; boundless energy and enthusiasm; a willingness to stand up for yourself and go for what you want; a feeling of trust in the universe and in others; good supportive relationships and bags of confidence. Yes we really do sparkle and shine when the sun is out in our life.

For more than twenty years I have worked as a trainer, counsellor and life coach. My clients have come from all strata of society including the rich and famous; the bereaved; the poor and unemployed; disaffected teenagers and people just like you. This might be hard to believe but it is certainly true that every single client with whom I have worked has wanted one thing above all others: *everyone* thinks that their life would change for the better if only they had more confidence! Confidence brings irrepressible self-belief and a fabulous feeling of 'aliveness' and wellbeing; no wonder it is at the top of every client's wish-list!

For as long as I can remember I have been fascinated by the energy and charisma that surrounds a person who is confident and sure of themselves. As a child I would notice those people who always seemed one step ahead of the rest and appeared somewhat larger than life; I admired their poise and calm self-sufficiency; I could feel the powerful personal magnetism that they radiated and I wanted some of that amazing energy! Over the years my ongoing fascination with this subject has grown as I have discovered more and more self-empowering techniques (from the most ancient and traditional to those at the leading edge of personal development research). This passion of mine has developed into a long career of teaching, coaching and writing about all issues relating to our individual quests for the magical gift of confidence and all that it brings.

Elisabeth Kübler-Ross refers to the 'light within' which can sustain us even at our darkest moments. Here she is referring to the quality of spiritual lightness than comes with quiet inner conviction and inner confidence. Confidence has many faces and not all of them are super-assertive, go-getting and can-doing.

Weekend Confidence Coach takes you on a journey to find the truly confident you. Beyond your personal doubts and fears is a place where you are full of self-worth and high in self-respect. Here you can overcome any challenge and bounce back again and again. You are a fabulously strong and dynamic person with powerful inner resources that you can access whenever you need to. Why not decide to step into that magical circle of confidence and become your very best self?

Confidence can come and go within a moment so it is important to understand exactly how and why this happens and what we can do about it when it does. Those of you who are struggling with lack of self-belief and self-worth need to know that these issues can easily be resolved. You *can* get back on track again; you need only decide to make this your goal and then pursue that goal wholeheartedly.

Life coaching offers the most wonderful strategies for self-change and personal development and so I have applied the coaching framework to the issue of confidence. If self-confidence is your goal then make it your top priority. Find time that you can set aside to relax and focus on yourself, to the exclusion of all others. Make yourself a priority next weekend and have a 48-hour personal confidence coaching session.

Your goal is to step out of the wings and take the centre stage of your life. Get out there and be what you can be; do what you can do and reach for the very highest within yourself. You definitely have what it takes to sparkle with confidence and shine from within.

Part One

SEVEN STEPS TO BEING YOUR OWN CONFIDENCE COACH

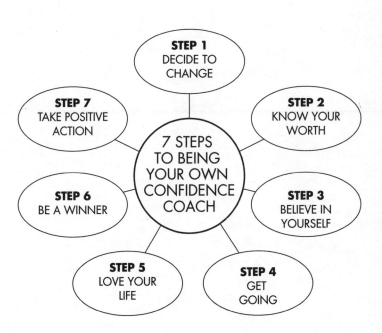

Introduction
A Confident New You

Only as high as I reach can I grow,
Only as far as I seek can I go,
Only as deep as I look can I see,
Only as much as I dream can I be.

KAREN RAVN

When we are brimming with self-confidence we are focused, motivated and feeling 'right' about things. That sense of certainty rubs off on to others who respond positively to our suggestions and so we attract good vibrant positive energy and draw success into our lives; it's easy! Well, it seems so when we are feeling confident, but when we are not then success can feel a million miles away.

We all know what is meant by the word confidence, but interestingly this meaning is different for everyone. Confidence can't be defined easily because it is a personal quality, but we can all agree on one thing: it makes us feel good. So confidence could be described as the 'feel-good factor which is based on self-belief'. And *Weekend Confidence Coach* is all about how you can inject more of this feel-good factor into your everyday life.

You might have bought this book because you would like to feel more sure of yourself in a particular area of your life. Perhaps you need to be more assertive at work or maybe more confident in your relationships. If you are shy and find it hard to socialise then you could certainly do with a boost to your self-esteem. Or you might be struggling to get out of a comfort zone, even when you know that it is high time for a change. We all find change difficult but if you are low in self-belief then you will be doubting your ability both to create new goals and also to go for them.

One of the symptoms of low self-confidence is a seemingly unshakeable belief that everyone you see around you is self-assured; they know what they are doing and where they are going; they are strong and focused and have no self-doubts. Perhaps the most important thing that I can tell you is that *this is an illusion.* When our self-esteem is at rock bottom we naturally slip into a negative cycle where we believe that we are *not as good as* whoever it is we are comparing ourselves with. It's so easy to fall into this trap, particularly on a day when we are not feeling at our attractive best. On such a day a mere flip through a glossy magazine can be all it takes to send us into the doom and gloom of a body confidence crisis.

Weekend Confidence Coach takes an in-depth look at confidence and all the issues associated with it. It considers such questions as: Why do we choose to give ourselves such a hard time? How can we learn to be kinder to ourselves and to demonstrate the self-respect that we deserve? Is it possible to step out of the low-confidence habit; to leave self-doubts behind and to become strong and clear about what we want and don't want in our lives? How can we reach beyond our self-limiting beliefs and realise our true potential? What can we do to lift ourselves out of a negative cycle and into a positive one?

My experience of working on the self-confidence issue

with many hundreds of clients leads me to a wonderful and uplifting conclusion. If confidence is your goal then you can certainly go for it and achieve it. Everything changes and you can change too. I have seen so many miraculous trans-formations where people have turned what they felt to be a mediocre and humdrum life into one that blazes and sparkles with energy, zest and enthusiasm. Rise above your doubts: reach for your highest dreams and watch them unfold before your very eyes. I know that you can do this; all it takes is for you to know it too.

How to use *Weekend Confidence Coach*

Allocate some time alone to work through this book. If you can take advantage of a relaxed low-key weekend then so much the better, but if you feel like you are juggling a whole dinner service (let alone a few plates!) then it is definitely time to make time for yourself! Gaining the confidence to be yourself begins with the recognition that you deserve to relax and evaluate your own needs. This might mean restructuring your day so that you have a few uninterrupted hours. Do you need to delegate chores or ask for help with childcare? Perhaps you just need to let go of any task that is not top priority. Do whatever it takes so that you can put yourself first for once! Finding time for yourself is one of the very first steps you will need to take if you are really serious about becoming more confident.

You might like to buy a notebook to use as a journal so that you can keep track of your ongoing thoughts and reflections. And then all you need to do is to sit back and relax and get reading.

Weekend Confidence Coach is intended to be upbeat,

positive and dynamic and so will you be when you read it. My coaching methods are encouraging, supportive and motivating. I take a calm and relaxed approach to self-change because this is the only method that really works. People change from the inside out, which means that there is always inner work to be done before we can alter our behaviour. When we act confidently it is because we have powerful inner convictions and a strong sense of self. Throughout the book you will find 'Instant Boosts' that offer quick and easy ways to raise your energy and your levels of confidence. And every chapter contains 'Inner Reflections', which will allow you to really relax and let go. In this calm, centred and focused space you will discover just how easy it is to be the person you most want to be: confident, self-assured; happy; relaxed and stress-free.

Part One of this book is an easy step-by-step guide to becoming more confident, assertive and self-assured. Simply follow these steps and you will very quickly begin to feel more in charge of yourself, your feelings and your behaviour.

Step 1: Decide to Change shows you how to do just that! You have bought this book because you want to make changes in your life and you know what those changes are. So get clear about what you want and why. Assess what confidence really means to you, reflect on your conclusions and be ready to take a stand. As soon as you begin to look your life in the eye you are already making an important assertive statement about yourself: you are saying here I am and I am going to take control. You are in charge; just believe this.

Step 2: Know Your Worth and your true value. Yes,

you will face many challenges but with a positive approach you can always find the inner strength you need. Learn what it takes to stay in the cycle of success and you will stay cool and calm and ready to deal with whatever life throws at you.

Step 3: Believe in Yourself reminds you that you can really go for your goals; there is nothing holding you back except yourself. Review your self-image; confront your self-doubts and decide to change, now. And as soon as you start to focus on what you *can* do (rather than focusing on what you can't do) an amazing thing happens: you begin to believe in yourself! It becomes simple to take the first easy step towards a goal and then, before you know it, you are motivated, energised and on your way. What are you waiting for?

Step 4: Get Going. You can do whatever you want to do as long as you are passionate enough about your goals. With a 'can-do' approach anything is possible so take that risk and name your dream. Go-getters are not people pleasers, they know what they want and they follow through for themselves. The right time is now so stop procrastinating and just get going.

Step 5: Love Your Life shows the link between happiness and confidence. Success is not just about coming first or having things turn out right all the time. Life is a roller-coaster and real confidence depends on your ability to ride the ups and downs and still keep smiling. Confident people know that it is not what happens to them that matters most, rather it is how they deal with what happens. When you can love and appreciate each precious moment of your life you will become more positive, optimistic and serene.

Step 6: **Be a Winner** by reaching for the very best in yourself and others. When you know that you have given your best shot then whatever happens you will feel a sense of self-respect; a life well-lived is a fast-track route to confidence and strong self-belief. You carry your thoughts and feelings about yourself wherever you go and others pick up on the vibrations that you give off. When you are confident and at ease you attract the very best that life offers. So get into that positive cycle of success.

Step 7: **Take Positive Action** explains how we really do create our own reality. When you take full responsibility for yourself you stop being a victim and you will be amazed by the effect this has in every single aspect of your life. Your relationships will improve and you will start to attract optimistic and upbeat people into your orbit. Taking charge will give your confidence a massive boost and will fill you with the motivation and energy you need to go for some exciting new goals.

Let these seven steps provide a framework for you to fall back on whenever your confidence takes a nosedive and you are feeling low in self-esteem and struggling to find a positive slant. You can check that you are keeping to these guidelines by asking yourself the following questions:

- Am I clear about what I want? Am I standing up for myself and telling the truth?

- Do I recognise my true worth and my inner strength?
- Am I focusing on what I can do rather than on what I can't do?
- Am I expressing my real needs and are those needs being met by others?
- Do I really appreciate my life or am I moaning and complaining and bringing myself and everyone else down?
- Are my natural talents and charms shining through? Am I living my life wholeheartedly and giving of my best?
- Am I taking responsibility for the quality of my life or am I acting like a victim?

Use the tips, tools and strategies in Part One to become your own confidence coach and so upgrade the quality of your life. Begin to believe in yourself and you will find that everything feels more possible.

Part Two demonstrates how your increasing self-awareness leads to a clear understanding of what it takes to live a truly confident life. It shows you exactly how to maintain high confidence levels in all areas of your life.

Make an Impact shows you how to make a strong and lasting impression on others. Some people appear naturally charismatic and appealing and you can be like this too once you learn the art of positive projection. A woman with a positive self-image is intent on becoming a first-rate version of herself. She knows that she is special and unique and never compares herself unfavourably with others. Learn how to tap into your powerful personal magnetism and demonstrate your strength of character to all who meet you; become a shining star.

Be an Optimist demonstrates that you can only exude an air of calm self-confidence when you are ready to drop the pessimistic, negative front and are willing to embrace optimism. Cynics can never win the big prizes or make close emotional bonds so why not go for the totally positive approach? Confident people have an optimistic and realistic approach to life. They trust themselves and they trust the universe; they expect the best and they live prosperously. When you decide to be happy you attract powerful positive energy into all areas of your life. Believe me, optimists have learned their art and you can too!

Go with the Flow encourages you to look at the bigger picture of your life so that you are able to feel a sense of meaning and purpose in all that you do. Our lives can be so driven and hectic that we often forget to stop and value the moment. Tearing towards the future or looking back with regret we can miss the most important thing of all: the experience of the now, this precious moment. When you can recognise the spiritual element of your being you will realise what you are really worth! You are so much more than you appear to be and as we look beyond the material level you will discover amazing depths and insights.

Change Your Life explains how having the confidence to make lifestyle changes depends on two important issues. We need to recognise and understand the psychology of self-change and we need to increase our personal levels of self-awareness. Knowledge is power, so get to know just how you tick. Learn how to get SMART about your goals and how to create a foolproof action plan.

As your self-belief increases your expectations will rise. We always attract the circumstances and the people that we think we deserve, so as you develop in confidence you will automatically change your life for the better. But don't just accept that this is true, go ahead and prove it to yourself.

Go for confidence with 100 per cent effort. Don't hold back, give it all you have got: let total confidence be your goal. You have taken the first step by buying *Weekend Confidence Coach* and demonstrating your powerful intention to change. Now take the next step and read the rest of the book. This is the beginning of an exciting new start for you; enjoy the process of change and admire your inner strength and perseverance. Get focused, be committed and go for the super-confident new you!

Step 1
Decide to Change

We have witnessed time and again on our television programmes and in our clothing workshops how looking good can change a woman's life. In filming our most recent series for BBC1 we have learned more about women of different ages and lifestyles than ever before. We have lived the lives of mothers with toddlers and teenage daughters, women going through a midlife crisis, the loneliness of the woman looking for Mr Commitment, and the scariness of the menopause . . . we have been able to understand how very confusing it can be for women moving on to another stage of their life, how all-consuming are the physical and emotional changes that we have to go through during the course of our lives.

TRINNY WOODALL AND
SUSANNAH CONSTANTINE

Trinny and Susannah certainly take no hostages; they have a tough no-nonsense bootcamp approach, and they get results. Their TV shows and books have become immensely popular because they are so straightforward and to the point. Speaking of their book *What You Wear Can Change Your Life*, they say,

'This book is not a retouched glossy magazine account of the road to perfection. It is the honest and truthful story of how to look at yourself and see what you can make better.'

What you wear can certainly make you feel better about yourself and Trinny and Susannah are doing a wonderful job working directly with women on their body confidence issues. Many of my own clients struggle to accept the bodily gifts with which they are endowed and this daily challenge certainly can affect their personal levels of self-esteem.

I appreciate the value of looking good, and believe me I know how easy it is to let a bad hair day bring you down. But body confidence; good dress sense; gorgeous flattering make-up; a Nicky Clarke haircut and a fabulous pair of Jimmy Choos are not all it takes to bring a feeling of calm self-assuredness into our lives. As our two fashion gurus have noted, we are all continually facing extraordinary physical and emotional changes and these challenge us at the very deepest level.

Weekend Confidence Coach is also an honest and truthful story of how to look at yourself and see what you can make better. But here we will be looking at a total confidence package that spans all aspects of your life. Body confidence is important but then so is relationship confidence. On the one hand your love life might be great, but on the other you may be stuck in a career rut. Or maybe you are struggling with being able to speak to strangers or with expressing your feelings to loved ones. Stop here and take a moment to think about why you bought this book. Where would you like to feel more certain and sure of yourself? How would your life change if you could boost your self-esteem? If your self-worth increased can you imagine the knock-on effects that this would have?

The act of looking at yourself to see what you can make

better requires a strong commitment to change: it means being utterly realistic and ready to take a stand and say, 'This is who I am, this is what I want and this is what I will do to achieve it.' Have no doubt that if you sincerely intend to change then you will.

I am always telling clients that they must be in love with their goals if they are going to reach them. So how passionate are you about bringing a new level of confidence into your life? How motivated are you to raise your self-esteem? On a scale of 1–10 give yourself a passion score now. If you gave yourself a score of 9 or below then pass this book on to someone else who is ready to use it. If you gave yourself 10 then, make no mistake, you have decided to change and you are absolutely ready to take the next step towards total confidence; let's go!

Confidence is . . .

- Being able to see the good in others.
- Taking responsibility for your thoughts and actions.
- Letting go of blame.
- Knowing that the dark clouds will pass.
- Believing in yourself even when you have made a mistake.
- Telling the truth about how you feel and taking appropriate action.
- Looking for the silver lining in every challenging situation.
- Taking care of yourself both physically and emotionally.
- Knowing where to draw your line in the sand and standing by your decision.
- Keeping a sense of humour.
- Accepting human weaknesses.

- Moving on from the past.
- Bouncing back from setbacks.
- Radiating positivity and shining with inner strength.
- Forgiving yourself and others.
- Embracing all of life and living wholeheartedly.
- Supporting and appreciating other people.
- Loving and valuing yourself.
- Keeping things in perspective.
- Feeling free to be yourself.

EXERCISE:

What does confidence mean to you?

Confidence is such a personal issue and we all have our own individual take on what it means to us. When you have completed the following statements you will have more idea of the type of changes you will need to make in order to increase your levels of inner security and confidence.

1 When I am feeling confident I am . . . .
2 Self-doubt makes me . . . .
3 My self-worth is high when . . . .
4 I know that I am right when . . . .
5 I am at my best in relationships when . . . .
6 I lose confidence in myself when . . . .
7 When I am facing a big challenge I . . . .
8 If I make a mistake I feel . . . .
9 If someone criticises me I feel . . . .
10 Increasing my self-confidence would make it possible for
   me to . . . .

Take a stand

Self-belief removes doubt and brings a wonderful clarity to our daily life; we go with the flow and seem to know intuitively which step to take next. We draw this feeling of 'rightness' into our lives whenever we decide to take a stand. Of course there are times when it's good to lay out all our possibilities and wait to act until the time feels right. But sometimes we can let that magic moment pass and find ourselves trapped in uncertainty, procrastination and self-doubt.

Justine's story

Justine, 32, is in marketing and loves her job. Last year her boss took early retirement and a new woman took her place. Her new boss (who we will call Julia) came into the job with a 'new broom sweeps clean' approach; she wanted to make big changes and she did so without referring to the team she was supervising. For six months Justine went along with Julia who gave her more and more administrative duties and fewer and fewer responsibilities. This meant that Justine virtually stopped dealing directly with clients and this had been the part of the job that she loved the most. By the time we met Justine felt flat and fed-up and stressed. She said that she no longer felt useful at work and that she dreaded going in each morning. But of course she had to keep paying the bills and so she felt trapped by the situation.

Justine had plenty of complaints but when she had aired them all I asked her what she wanted to happen. Life coaching helps clients to look realistically and positively at their situation, whatever it is. When life gets hard it's often easier to use our precious energy moaning and blaming, but of course this never creates a new outcome. The more we talk about what we don't like the less able we are to focus on the ways and means of bringing about constructive change. So Justine was quite floored by this simple question. I asked her to go away and think about it. Three days later I received an email saying that she had decided that she was ready to tackle Julia head-on to tell her how she felt. Justine wrote, 'I really don't know why I have let this situation go on for so long. I think I feel intimidated by Julia who has an MBA from Harvard Business School and always seems so articulate and in control. I didn't even go to university and although I know this job inside and out I have always felt my lack of higher education. But I'm good at my job and I'm ready to say my piece whatever the consequences and if nothing changes I'll go and work for another agency (there are plenty around who might take me on). Actually now I've decided to do something for myself I feel much more confident and self-assured. I let Julia intimidate me from the start and if I could have been more assertive back then it would probably never have got to this stage.'

Once Justine recognised her own worth in the workplace she was able to strand up for herself without fear. And in the end her relationship with Julia changed and became more amicable. Justine began to deal directly with the clients once more and she is now thinking of taking an Open University course.

When we find ourselves being treated badly we need to look past our victimiser. *(Yes this person is taking me for granted, but why am I letting them?)* Whenever you are low in confidence you are face-to-face with your own self-doubt. As soon as you start to believe in yourself again the ground shifts and you find that others begin to treat you with more respect. Whenever you take a stand you are saying to other people, 'This is who I am, this is what I want and I am worth it!' Try it; it works like a dream every time.

INNER REFLECTION

ENJOY THE 'NOW'

STOP AND RELAX FOR A MOMENT. PUT THE BOOK DOWN AND PUT YOUR FEET UP AND JUST EXPERIENCE THE QUIET CALM OF THIS PERFECT MOMENT. LET GO OF YOUR WORRIES ABOUT THE FUTURE AND REGRETS ABOUT THE PAST AND BRING YOUR AWARENESS INTO THE 'NOW'.

IN THIS PRESENT MOMENT THERE IS PEACE AND CALM AND SERENITY. STAY IN THE 'NOW' FOR AS LONG AS YOU CAN AND NOTICE THAT YOU ONLY LOSE YOUR COMPOSURE WHEN YOU START TO THINK OUTSIDE OF THE PRESENT MOMENT. WHEN THINGS GET TOO MUCH YOU CAN ALWAYS FIND YOUR CALM CENTRE BY CONCENTRATING ON EXPERIENCING THIS SINGLE PRECIOUS MOMENT OF YOUR LIFE.

Shine with inner conviction

As soon as you take a stand you are making a clear decision and following a conscious choice. This means that you take yourself and your decisions seriously and that you trust your own integrity and are ready to follow through with whatever it takes. In other words you are saying what you really mean and staying on your own side at all times. You will immediately recognise a person who is taking a stand in this way. Their inner strength and conviction shine through, however dire their circumstances.

At the very moment I am writing this my mother-in-law, Mary Field, is lying in hospital in an acute stroke ward; a place filled with both misery and grace. Many of the patients stand only a very small chance of even partial recovery and they and their visitors endure a hard struggle to keep positive and confident in the face of a poor prognosis.

I spent Christmas on this ward, surrounded by nurses who were just like real angels. I also met Lottie, a remarkable woman who is 101 years old. Two weeks ago she lived in her own house and managed all her own affairs and then she had a stroke and lost the use of her legs. Lottie drew me like a magnet and I spent many hours with her listening to her delightful stories of a bygone age. She is a woman with courage and charisma and extraordinary energy and although she woke at night with nightmares about never being able to walk again she was determined to rise to this enormous challenge. Yesterday I came home and when my husband phoned from the hospital he told me that Lottie had taken three steps to tremendous applause on the ward. This amazing woman had given me strength when I most needed it. She was caring and kind with a courageous self-confidence that rubbed off on everyone she spoke with. And she really did literally take a stand when it had seemed a total impossibility.

Never doubt that you have the courage you need to step forward to make the very best of your life. The human spirit is strong and serene and you can trust yourself at the deepest level. Be brave and follow your heart and make your dreams come true; if Lottie can take a stand then we can too!

INSTANT BOOST

MAKE A FRESH START EVERY DAY

You can rise to your challenges whatever they might be. But maybe you are feeling daunted by what this will entail. If so just try this technique, which will ensure that you wake each morning with a clean slate, hopeful and ready to do the best that you can.

- When you wake up take a few minutes to consider the day ahead.
- Think about the wonderful changes that you are going to bring about and fill yourself with inspiration.
- Before you go to sleep take a few minutes to complete the day and review all the choices you made.
- Congratulate yourself for all the positivity and courage that you have shown.
- And if you feel that you have let yourself down in any way, give yourself a break and another chance to get it right.
- In this way you allow yourself a fresh and optimistic start each and every day.

Total confidence does not require perfection

When I speak about total confidence I am not referring to a glossy image of perfection. There is actually no such thing as a totally confident person; we are always changing and growing; nothing stays the same and we are continually challenged to keep flexible. Total confidence is not so much a state of being but rather it is a state of mind.

A classic symptom of low self-confidence is a compulsion to go comparison shopping (an activity which is just as addictive as the high street variety). Comparison shopping happens when we feel low in self-esteem and so begin to match ourselves against more beautiful, more talented and more highly intelligent others, all of whom personify wellbeing, confidence and chutzpah. As our self-worth drops we want to escape our own feelings and so we look outside ourselves for the gifts we think we seek. And of course we see brilliance, talent and beauty everywhere we look; everyone looks more together than we feel. Our insecurity ensures that we always fall to the bottom of the pile in this exercise and this further reinforces our self-doubt and lack of confidence. Whenever we are feeling 'not good enough' we look to other people who we consider *are* good enough and so we are always found lacking. If you don't think that you have ever indulged in this activity then think again. Next time you feel intimidated, embarrassed or inadequate just stop and notice that this feeling is never only about you; it is *always* about how you see yourself in relation to others! Look at the diagram over the page to see how this works.

Clients and workshop participants often want to know how to be confident and happy all the time. But of course I

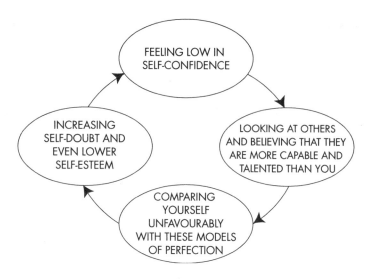

FEELING LOW IN
SELF-CONFIDENCE

LOOKING AT OTHERS
AND BELIEVING THAT THEY
ARE MORE CAPABLE AND
TALENTED THAN YOU

COMPARING
YOURSELF
UNFAVOURABLY
WITH THESE MODELS
OF PERFECTION

INCREASING
SELF-DOUBT AND
EVEN LOWER
SELF-ESTEEM

COMPARISON SHOPPING

can't tell them how to do this because our human life embraces all emotions, the ups as well as the downs. Circumstances and people are unpredictable; everyone experiences getting what they don't want some of the time! We know that this is true and yet we still hang on to a strong belief that if only we could get everything right (be perfect, always be good enough, etc.) we would be safe and secure for the rest of our lives. This is an illusion and as soon as we grasp this we are well on our way to understanding how to live a confident life.

Total confidence only comes when we change our attitude to the way we view our lives and ourselves. If we try to run a competitive race with other people we will always lose in the end. The only way to stay centred and secure is to base our relationships on trust and co-operation and in this way we can respect our own worth as well as the worth of others.

EXERCISE

You are what you believe you are

1 Sit quietly for a few moments and relax your body and your mind. Take some slow and deep breaths and feel yourself unwind. Now, go back to a time when you were feeling high in self-esteem and full of self-respect; it doesn't matter how long ago this was. Close your eyes and see yourself in this confident, decisive and relaxed mode. Try to remember the details of this experience. Where were you? Who was with you? What did you feel like? Recapture those feelings right now; recreate that sense of feeling great and in the flow. The world feels fabulous, doesn't it? Now, ask yourself: *what do I believe about myself?* . . . .

. . . .

. . . .

2 Close your eyes again and imagine a situation where you were low in self-esteem; your confidence was at rock bottom. It probably won't be very hard to remember exactly what this felt like. Now, feel the painful emotions as clearly as possible and ask yourself: *what do I believe to be true about myself now?* . . . .

. . . .

. . . .

3 Come back to the present moment and ask yourself: *which set of beliefs is true?* . . . .

. . . .

. . . .

If we can have opposing beliefs about ourselves at different times then obviously our beliefs must be changeable. This has important implications, which we will be looking at later.

Become a decision-maker

The happiest people I know are those who can trust their own decisions. When confidence is low we lose faith in our own judgement and then it can seem impossible to know what to do next, what to say and even what to believe. At a time like this it is good to have something to fall back on which will help to clarify your thoughts and refocus your energy.

Next time you are unsure about which decision to make don't automatically get into a flap, which will only make you more confused. As soon as indecision strikes, hit back with this great life coaching strategy:

- **Establish your intention.** In other words, clarify your outcome. What is it that you want to happen here? Once you know your intention you can work backwards to discover exactly *how* you can achieve it.
- **Create an action plan.** Once you know what you are going for you can determine the first step that you must take. Ask yourself how you can achieve your outcome.
- **Take the first step towards your goal.** What do you need to do to get going? Stop deliberating and procrastinating and JUST DO IT!

Use this assertive, go-getting technique whenever indecisiveness floors you. Remember that confidence is all about attitude and if you can maintain a positive approach in the face of indecision you will always rise above self-doubt.

When confidence levels fall (for whatever reason) it is all too easy to go down into a negative cycle of helplessness and hopelessness. *Look at me I can't even make a simple*

*decision, I'm hopeless, no good, I give up, I have lost control
. . . etc.* We all know what this feels like but we don't have to
indulge our negative responses, we can rise out of this black
mood. Just take a step back and implement this strategy; get
going and take control of your life; you can do this!

Your heartfelt intention

What do I want to happen? is the question that gets to the
very heart of the decision-making process. Writing in *O
Magazine,* Oprah Winfrey suggests that, 'Before you agree to
do anything that might add even the smallest amount of
stress to your life, ask yourself: What is my truest intention?
Give yourself time to let a yes resound within you. When it's
right, I guarantee that your entire body will feel it.'

Often clients grapple with an intellectual process when I
first ask them what they would like to happen; they might
talk about the pros and cons of taking this or that action and
maybe write a list of fors and againsts. This is certainly a good
start but it is only a start. Actually I have never known anyone
to make a decision based purely on the facts. Our choices are
made at a much deeper level; we are guided by our hearts as
well as our heads. Our intention demands a level of commitment and we can only fulfil that obligation if we feel the
sense of rightness that Oprah talks about.

Just think back to a time when you made a bad decision
(we all make these all of the time so don't get stuck in self-
criticism here). Employ an air of detachment and just clearly
assess *how* you made the decision. Perhaps you made a poor
choice because you didn't have access to all the facts. Or
maybe you just didn't know what you were walking into. Or
possibly you were wearing your rose-tinted specs because

you so wanted to believe something that you actually did have some reservations about. Try to remember how you felt about this decision. Did it feel 'right' or were you unsure?

Now look at how you made one of your really great decisions. How did you tap into your truest intention? Did you feel a yes (or a no) resound within you? It doesn't matter if you can't put this feeling into words, you only need to know how to recognise your gut instincts and then to have the courage to follow them. You can always recognise your real intention because it calls to you from a place within that *knows* what is good for you and what is harmful. Throughout this book we will be returning again and again to the issue of your heartfelt intention because confidence stems from *knowing* what you want at the very deepest level.

Stop! Give yourself a break

In a recent interview, Michelle Collins (former star of *EastEnders*) talked about her past struggle with anorexia and low confidence and had this to say: 'People say it takes a traumatic event to become anorexic, but I'm not sure that's true. For me, it was to do with low self-esteem. It might even be to do with having an addictive personality. I am a perfectionist. I'm very critical of myself. If someone says something negative about me, I give myself such a hard time. I'll have endless conversations in my head and I analyse myself to the point where I have to say: "Stop! Give yourself a break."'

Yes, even glamourous and successful stars can find themselves locked in a negative cycle where they feel 'not good enough' in some way. Maybe you can relate to some of the points that Michelle makes. Are you striving for perfection in any area of your life? If you are you have set yourself up for certain failure and misery. How can we expect so much of ourselves and yet allow others the benefit of the doubt every time? Would you ever dream of treating a friend to the sort of roasting that you give yourself when you have not fulfilled your highest self-expectations?

You are your own sternest critic and you will never feel self-confident until you can stop and give yourself a break. We can take this self-criticism to the realms of the absurd without even realising it. I have even known clients who have been working hard on their self-development start to criticise themselves for their lack of progress. If you are recognising yourself here just relax and know that you are in fine company; to some degree we *all* indulge in self-critical analysis. One of the main purposes of this book is to demonstrate how easy it is to ditch the never-ending self-recriminations and to learn how to love and encourage ourselves. The feeling of total confidence allows us to embrace our mistakes and so-called 'failures'; it recognises that we are always learning, developing and growing and it supports us when we are feeling low about our world and ourselves.

The next time you are feeling criticised, hurt or rejected (whether it is by someone else or simply self-imposed) remember to stop your neurotic ramblings and give yourself a break. Don't let that inner critical voice ruin your day. Stand firm and remember who you are; you are amazing so let yourself be amazing. Smile at yourself and remember that you are here for a purpose and it is a much greater one than indulging in self-reproach. Step out of the dark critical trap and into the sunshine of your life.

INNER REFLECTION

TOUCH AND GO

TRY THIS RATHER BEAUTIFUL BUDDHIST INSTRUCTION, WHICH IS CALLED 'TOUCH AND GO'.

- CLOSE YOUR EYES, RELAX YOUR BODY AND MIND AND BREATHE DEEPLY AND EASILY.
- NOW BECOME AWARE OF THE CONSTANT CHATTER OF YOUR MIND, NOTICE THE THOUGHTS RUSHING PAST – THE MIND IS NEVER STILL.
- RATHER THAN TRY TO STOP YOUR THOUGHTS JUST TAKE THE ROLE OF THE OBSERVER AND WATCH THEM PASS BY.
- TOUCH YOUR THOUGHTS BY ACKNOWLEDGING THEM, BUT DON'T ALLOW YOURSELF TO GET INVOLVED IN ANY WAY.
- AS SOON AS YOU HAVE TOUCHED A THOUGHT YOU CAN LET IT GO – TOUCH AND GO!
- THIS EASY AND LIGHT MEDITATION HAS BEEN DESCRIBED AS BEING LIKE TOUCHING A BUBBLE WITH A FEATHER.
- SIT FOR A FEW MINUTES JUST TOUCHING AND LETTING GO OF YOUR THOUGHTS.
- WHEN YOU ARE READY OPEN YOUR EYES AND NOTICE HOW RELAXED YOU FEEL.

TRY USING THE TOUCH AND GO TECHNIQUE DURING YOUR DAILY BUSINESS. WHEN YOU NOTICE A CRITICAL THOUGHT JUST TOUCH IT (NO ANALYSIS, NO JUDGEMENT) AND THEN LET IT PASS BY.

Step 2
Know Your Worth

I wanted to become famous to prove I was a worthy person, but eventually I realised only you can make yourself feel worthy.

DAVINA MCCALL

There is an exercise I sometimes use in my workshops called, 'How much is it worth?' In this activity participants are asked to imagine that they have been approached by someone with limitless wealth who would like to buy just one day of their life. The promise is that the day would never actually be used for anything but would be locked away and never spoken of or acknowledged again. The buyer can choose any future day and they only have to name their price.

There is always a range of responses. Someone might consider selling a day for a vast amount of money, another would accept much less and some say that they would never ever dream of selling a day for any price. Consider this proposal yourself. What would you charge for one day of your life? How much is it worth? For example you might think it worth giving up a day for £10 million because you feel that such an amount would change your life. Or perhaps you would ask for an even bigger sum so that you could use it to help others. Or maybe you would never ever put a price on twenty-four hours of your life.

Whether you sold your day for say, £10 million, or whether you didn't sell it because it is beyond price, the most important points are these:

- Was today a priceless day?
- Was it a £10 million day?
- Did you live it to the absolute limit?
- Did you take every chance that this last twenty-four hours has offered you?
- Did you appreciate and value the gift of your day?
- Was today worth a day of your life?

Perhaps you had a worrying and troubling day and would gladly have paid someone to have it instead. It is true that some days are challenging and hard to live; we all have to go through times like these. But the full experience of life always involves us in difficulty as well as reward and the only way to deal with this is to know how to value yourself and your life at every single moment. Take a few quiet moments to think about how much you value your own worth.

INSTANT BOOST

LIVING A PRICELESS DAY

AS SOON AS WE WAKE WE ARE ON THE GO, BUSY AND PREOCCUPIED WITH FULFILLING OUR DAILY TASKS. TOO OFTEN WE ALLOW OUR HECTIC LIVES TO TAKE OVER SO THAT OUR PRECIOUS MOMENTS BECOME ORDINARY AND EVEN MUNDANE AND BORING.

YOUR DAY IS WORTH EXACTLY THE VALUE THAT YOU BRING TO IT, SO WHY NOT START TO INCREASE ITS VALUE? TRY THE FOLLOWING:

- **LOOK FOR THINGS TO APPRECIATE:** A BEAUTIFUL SUNSET, A SMILE FROM A STRANGER, THE CONSIDERATION OF A COLLEAGUE, THE THOUGHTFULNESS OF A FRIEND, A BIRD SINGING FOR ALL THAT IT'S WORTH..., SUCH THINGS BRING A DEEP SATISFACTION TO THE SOUL, SO TAKE CARE TO NOTICE THE MEANINGFUL MOMENTS THAT FILL YOUR LIFE.

- **RECOGNISE WHAT BRINGS YOU JOY** AND PURSUE THESE ACTIVITIES. DO YOU LOVE TO DANCE OR GO TO THE OPERA? WOULD YOU LIKE TO LEARN TO PAINT WITH WATERCOLOURS? OR HAVE YOU A BOOK THAT YOU ARE LONGING TO WRITE? WHY ARE YOU LIMITING YOUR JOYFUL MOMENTS? MAKE SURE THAT YOU GIVE TIME TO THE THINGS THAT BRING YOU JOY OR YOUR LIFE WILL NEVER FEEL TRULY WORTHWHILE. DO MORE OF THE THINGS YOU LOVE TO DO AND YOUR DAYS WILL BE TRANSFORMED.

- **THROUGHOUT THE DAY TAKE TIME TO STAND AND STARE.** A PRICELESS DAY NEEDS TO BE FREQUENTLY APPRECIATED. AT LEAST ONCE AN HOUR STOP, WHEREVER YOU ARE, AND JUST TAKE THE TIME TO BE GLAD TO BE ALIVE. THIS SOUNDS SO SIMPLE BUT IN FACT IT IS THE THING THAT WE ARE MOST LIKELY TO OVERLOOK.

- **BE THANKFUL FOR YOUR DAY.** BECOME AWARE OF ALL THAT BRINGS YOU SATISFACTION AND BE GLAD FOR WHAT YOU HAVE.

YOUR LIFE IS PRICELESS, JUST BE SURE TO REMEMBER THIS. THE MORE YOU CAN LOVE YOUR LIFE THE MORE IT WILL LOVE YOU BACK; TRY IT!

Don't be affected by what others think about you

The value we place on our life exactly reflects the value that we put on ourself. On a day when things are ticking along nicely it is easier to feel good about ourselves than when things are not going so well. On an upbeat day we project confidence and enthusiasm and others respond to our positive energy: yes we are feeling great and everyone else appreciates us. However, on a more difficult day our energy is withdrawn and less attractive; we might be feeling self-critical and others will probably not seem so supportive and appreciative.

The most important thing to remember *in either situation* is that what others think about you has no effect on your own self-image! If you wallow in the admiration of others on a good day then you will feel bereft without it on a bad day. Your intrinsic self-worth can never be allowed to be affected by the opinion of others.

Suzanne's story

Suzanne, 41, single mother and part-time piano teacher, was struggling with very low self-esteem. When she came for coaching my first question was, 'What would you like to achieve?' and she replied, 'I want to feel a sense of self-worth again.'

Ten years before, Suzanne's husband had left her and their (then) three-year-old twins for a young secretary who worked in his company. He said that he had had enough of her total preoccupation with the children and that he felt he deserved more time and attention. She was devastated and spent the next five years struggling with her feelings of humiliation, anger, guilt and rock-bottom confidence. And then she told me about Peter: 'He was a man who swept into my life and just changed everything. I loved his energy and go-getting approach and suddenly everything seemed possible again; I felt loved and desired and that certainly increased my self-esteem. We had some great holidays together when the twins stayed with their father and I was on top of the world for a few months. Peter never got involved with the domestic side of my life and he hardly ever saw the children and this was OK at first. But I began to feel that I was leading two separate lives, one where I was Peter's girlfriend and the other where I was a mother, homemaker and piano teacher. I broached the subject with Peter one night when he called around after the children had gone to bed, and he just hit the roof. He said that he wasn't into being "nagged", that the fun was going out of our relationship because I was getting too serious and that he had no intention of getting "saddled with someone else's brats". I backed down immediately and made things right again, and we carried on like this for a few weeks. But I felt changed and uneasy and it wasn't the same as before. And then, suddenly, I never saw him again; he just disappeared from my life.

'I fell into a deep pit of self-loathing and it was difficult to get up in the morning and to keep the children and my job together. I felt humiliated and despairing and I tried to contact Peter. But he changed his mobile number, and his secretary blocked all my calls to his workplace. I started to fall into a really depressed state where I felt a complete failure. It all seemed like a repeat of what happened when my husband left and I felt so dejected that my life didn't seem worth living.'

We met a couple of months later, after a client of mine had recommended me to Suzanne. Following our first session I encouraged Suzanne to make a more realistic assessment of her relationships with these two men. We also looked at her self-image and lack of self-worth. Over the next few weeks Suzanne began to let go of the guilt and anger that was helping to bring her down. For the first time she was able to see that neither of the relationship failures was totally her fault. When we lack self-esteem we are inclined to imagine that we are to blame for anything and everything that goes wrong (have you ever noticed how often you say 'sorry' when you are feeling low in confidence?).

Eventually Suzanne could clearly see that both her husband and Peter had something of the child about them; neither was willing to act like an adult in their relationship with Suzanne and both shied away from responsibility in favour of having 'fun'. Suzanne also began to respect herself for the great job she was doing bringing up the twins alone. She has decided to put her children first and to expand her teaching services as they get a bit older. At our last session Suzanne said, 'I feel so much better about myself now. I can't imagine why I ever doubted myself so much and why I let both those attention-seeking men bring me down. If I ever have another relationship it will be with a grown-up man who respects and admires who I am and the job I am doing keeping my family together.'

EXERCISE:

Because you are worth it

When we believe in ourselves and know our value we find it easy to make good decisions in every area of our life. Take a look at the statements on page 35 to see how your actions reveal your levels of self-worth.

INNER REFLECTION

APPRECIATE YOURSELF

RELAX, UNWIND AND OPEN YOUR HEART TO SELF-APPRECIATION. CONSIDER ALL THE WONDERFUL THINGS YOU HAVE DONE, YOUR COURAGE IN THE FACE OF ADVERSITY AND YOUR DETERMINATION AND GUTS. REMEMBER ALL THE OBSTACLES THAT YOU HAVE OVERCOME AND ADMIRE YOUR TENACITY. YOU ARE A WOMAN OF WORTH; TAKE THESE GOOD FEELINGS INTO YOUR DAILY LIFE.

STOP LOOKING FOR ADMIRATION AND APPLAUSE FROM OTHERS. BEGIN THIS IMMEDIATELY. START TO BECOME AWARE EACH TIME YOU ARE WAITING FOR SOMEONE ELSE TO SHOW YOU ESTEEM AND ASK YOURSELF WHY THEIR OPINION IS MORE IMPORTANT THAN YOURS. TRUST YOUR OWN JUDGEMENT.

Because I am worth it I . . .

- Am not afraid to look at my true feelings.
- Stand up for myself and never let anyone treat me badly.
- Walk away from victimisers and people who are not good for me.
- Enjoy my own company.
- Know that there is more to life than reaching a goal.
- Don't always have to be right.
- Let myself off when I make a mistake.
- Consider that my contribution is important; my input counts.
- Deserve to be treated with respect.

- Prioritise time with my family and loved ones.
- Refuse to tie myself up in guilty knots.
- Value my time and will not waste it in toxic relationships.
- Respect the fact that I will not always be at my best.
- Don't always need to be in control.
- Understand my need to relax and enjoy myself.
- Can take life as it comes, and go with the flow.

This list is not exhaustive and I am sure you can add many other statements that are right for you.

I am only too aware that these assertions describe someone who is feeling good and is high in self-esteem. I don't for one moment expect that you can tick all these items off right now. In fact who is that paragon of virtue who is always 100 per cent sure of their own worth and follows through in every instance? That person certainly isn't me and is unlikely to be you. When we look at such a list of virtues we know that we are only ever *working towards* such a state of total confidence.

Some self-help books have been rightly criticised for helping to create problems rather than helping to cure them. Journalist Cosmo Landesman, writing in the *Sunday Times* recently, has this to say: 'Nobody can be one of those fulfilled, self-controlling, happy, creative, goal-attaining demi-gods that exist in the world of self-help literature.'

He has a point and one that is important to raise here. When we reach for a book to help us increase our confidence we are most likely to be feeling less than our best. And when we see a list like the one above it is all too easy to throw our hands up in the air, chuck the book in the bin and turn on the telly. But everything changes, and we do too, and the most important issue here is that we learn how to make changes in a positive and open-hearted way rather than adopting behaviours that are negative and self-defeating. So as you work through the book keep reminding yourself that you are an amazing work in progress, ever-changing and developing. Every small positive step that you can take to bring more confidence into your life is a wonderful achievement and don't forget to acknowledge these steps. There are no 'goal-attaining demi-gods', only people like you and me who have our ups and downs and are trying to make the best of ourselves and our lives. **Because you are worth it** you deserve to keep reminding yourself of this important fact! Keep moving and take the positive path; this is what you deserve.

Look at it this way

No one escapes the challenges of life and, in fact, it has often been suggested that we become stronger in adversity. That's not to say that we need to go looking for trouble but we do need to know that, if it finds us, we don't have to fly straight into a negative and hopeless state. Looking back at a difficult twelve months, Jennifer Lopez says: 'It was a tough, transitional year, but I don't know if it was bad. It was a growing year. Things happened that haven't before and I believe they were meant for me. Look at where I am now. More alert, more happy, more alive. I appreciate things differently. You do after you have had a few knocks. You don't learn things through happy times.'

Consider some of your own past 'knocks'. How did you manage when the going got tough? When we are confronted with a new and difficult crisis we find that we can always depend on ourselves for the inner strength and courage that we need in order to cope. And when we look for more we always find more: more awareness, more understanding, more acceptance, more patience and more resolve. We are more amazing than we ever think we are; we are brave, determined and flexible, and sometimes it takes an emergency in order for us to recognise this.

As you reflect on your inner reserves begin to imagine how you could use these talents in your everyday life. Why wait for a disaster to strike before you show your best side? You are resourceful, creative and utterly capable; never forget to draw on these qualities whenever you need them.

The cycle of success

High self-worth attracts success, and low self-worth attracts defeat. At any one moment your degree of self-worth will reflect your confidence levels and will show in the ways that you think, act and feel.

When you believe in yourself and know your value, your thoughts, behaviour and feelings create a cycle of success that further enhances your self-worth. When you have a strong sense of self-belief you carry an unmistakable aura of confidence and wellbeing: you look good, feel good and sound good. And the more you believe in yourself the higher your self-expectations (you know without a doubt that you deserve the very best). Your behaviour is assertive and focused as you go for what you want unreservedly and this of course leads to increased feelings of self-confidence: success generates more success.

Think of a time when you were flowing in this cycle of success. Recollect how great you were feeling and how your

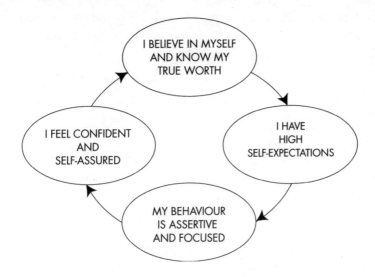

THE CYCLE OF SUCCESS

self-belief led you to a positive result and further enhanced your feelings of self-worth. Try to recall your actual thoughts, feelings and actions.

As soon as we allow our ourselves to believe that we are less than we are, we are indulging in self-doubt and this *always* leads into the cycle of defeat. The moment you query your self-worth is the moment that you lose your positive and optimistic feelings and fall into a negative cycle. When you lack self-belief this has an immediate knock-on effect: your self-expectations drop (how can I deserve the best when I am so useless, hopeless . . . etc.?) and this leads to unfocused and inappropriate behaviour, which increases your feelings of low self-confidence. Self-doubt only generates defeat.

I know that you know exactly how this cycle works; we have all experienced the colossal effects that self-doubt creates.

Can you remember a time when you found yourself caught

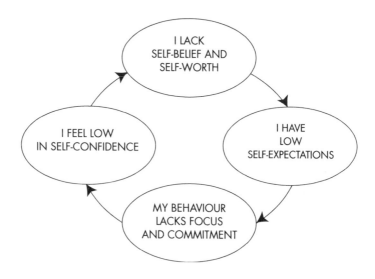

THE CYCLE OF DEFEAT

in the cycle of defeat? Perhaps you are feeling like this at the moment. If so please don't feel even more dejected, but recognise that the more clearly you can understand the way you think, feel and behave the easier it will be to move out of your predicament and into the positive cycle of success. This book is full of ideas and tips to help you to change the way you think and feel about yourself and the more self-aware you become the clearer your path to personal success.

People who are low in confidence are convinced that confident folk are 'lucky' or are 'born optimists'. I hope that it helps you to know that true confidence is achieved only by those who are prepared to do some work on themselves; there is very little luck involved. Admittedly some people have an easier start in life than others, but in the end all of us have to put the time in if we want to reach our true potential and have the confidence it takes to go for our dreams.

INSTANT BOOST

TAP INTO THE FEEL-GOOD FACTOR

SELF-DOUBT CAN STRIKE ANY OF US AT ANY TIME, MOVING US SWIFTLY FROM THE CYCLE OF SUCCESS INTO THE CYCLE OF DEFEAT.

BUT BECAUSE EMOTIONS ATTACH THEMSELVES TO MEMORIES, IT IS POSSIBLE TO CHANGE OUR MOOD BY RELIVING PAST RECOLLECTIONS OF SUCCESS, LOVE AND PLEASURE.

- THINK OF A PAST SUCCESS THAT FILLS YOU WITH PRIDE. REMEMBER HOW YOU FELT ABOUT YOUR ACHIEVEMENT AT THE TIME.
- BRING ALL THOSE GOOD FEELINGS BACK NOW BY RELIVING THE PAST. TAP INTO THOSE POSITIVE AND SUPER-CONFIDENT EMOTIONS AND BASK IN YOUR OWN GLORY.
- NOW THINK OF SOMEONE WHO LOVES YOU. IMAGINE THEM IN YOUR MIND'S EYE. FEEL HOW MUCH THEY CARE FOR YOU AND REMEMBER HOW MUCH YOU MEAN TO THEM; YOU ARE NEEDED AND VALUED.
- AND NOW RELIVE THE MEMORY OF A REALLY GOOD TIME. USE ANY 'HOOK' THAT WILL HELP YOU TO ENHANCE THE EXPERIENCE, SUCH AS PHOTOS OF THE OCCASION OR A PIECE OF MUSIC THAT WAS PLAYED.

SELF-DOUBT DISAPPEARS WHEN YOU START TO FEEL GOOD, SO TAP INTO YOUR MEMORY BANK, RELIVE YOUR POSITIVE FEELINGS AND REVIVE YOUR SELF-BELIEF.

A positive look at the past

Clients who struggle with self-confidence often refer to their past 'mistakes' and seem to dwell on their negative thoughts, feelings and behaviour. And although it is very important for us to look into our personal history so that we can know ourselves more clearly, it is vital that this search is done in a positive spirit. We can never progress and move on if we remain stuck in a negative view of our past. Self-criticism will always keep us going round and round in the cycle of defeat because the more we criticise ourselves the lower our self-worth falls.

When we can value our worth we can allow ourselves to make mistakes; in fact we can go further and decide actively to *learn* from those mistakes so that we never make them again. This attitude creates a powerful affirming take on our slip-ups and shortcomings, so that we no longer need to blame and punish ourselves each time we make an error.

You will notice that people who are low in confidence are always apologising for themselves and talking themselves 'down'; they are vocally self-critical and so project a very poor self-image (who could be inspired by someone who sets no value on their worth?). Alternatively you will notice that those who value themselves don't dwell on their short-comings and are enthusiastic and positive in their approach. Such people automatically gain the trust and support of others as they project a positive and assertive self-image.

EXERCISE:

Learning life's lessons

Think of a time when your attitude and behaviour created a negative outcome for you; in other words you didn't get what you wanted from a situation and you think the blame rests with you.

1 Describe the situation

. . . .
. . . .

2 What was the outcome you were hoping for?

. . . .
. . . .

3 What actually happened?

. . . .
. . . .

4 How did your attitude and behaviour affect the outcome? Be as specific as you can.

. . . .
. . . .

5 How would you change your attitude and behaviour if you were faced with a similar situation again?

. . . .
. . . .

6 What invaluable lessons did you learn from your mistakes?

. . . .
. . . .

Total confidence begins in the mind; you are always free to choose which attitude to take. If you take the negative, blaming, self-critical path you will always undervalue yourself and others; life will be an ongoing struggle and you will never feel truly confident. However, if you take the lighter, positive and more self-tolerant route you will be able to appreciate the true value of all human beings.

Every single person on the planet has an important and unique contribution to make. But each of us can only play our rightful part when we have finally recognised our own true worth.

INNER REFLECTION

MELT THAT MOUNTAIN

WE OFTEN CARRY OUR SELF-DOUBTS AND FEELINGS OF INADEQUACY LIKE PRECIOUS CARGO THAT WE MUST KEEP CHECKING AND THAT WE CAN NEVER PUT DOWN.

HOW MANY TIMES A DAY DO YOU GO OVER AND OVER THE REASONS WHY YOU CAN'T DO THIS OR THAT? HOW OFTEN DO YOU PICTURE YOURSELF FALLING AT THE NEXT HURDLE?

OUR THOUGHTS AND PICTURES HELP TO CREATE OUR FUTURE; IF WE FOCUS ON PROBLEMS AND BLOCKS, THEN WE DRAW EVEN MORE NEGATIVITY INTO OUR ORBIT. TRY THIS SIMPLE TECHNIQUE WHENEVER YOU FIND YOURSELF TIED UP IN A BELIEF OR A VISION THAT STOPS YOU GOING FOR YOUR GOAL.

- REFUSE TO TAKE THAT TORTUROUS SELF-CRITICAL ROUTE LEADING TO FAILURE.
- INTERRUPT ANY NEGATIVE THOUGHTS OR VISIONS WITH

THIS LITTLE VISUALISATION. IMAGINE THAT WHATEVER
IS STANDING IN YOUR WAY HAS TURNED INTO A BLOCK
OF ICE.

- NOW SEE YOURSELF WITH A GIANT HOSE OF HOT WATER
SIMPLY MELTING THE MOUNTAIN AWAY. THE BLOCK NO
LONGER EXISTS; YOU NEED NEVER THINK OF IT AGAIN.
YOUR PATH IS CLEAR AND YOU ARE FREE TO GO
FORWARD.

USE THIS VISUALISATION AT ANY MOMENT OF THE DAY
WHEN YOUR SELF-CONFIDENCE TAKES A KNOCK; MELT
THAT MOUNTAIN OF DOUBT AND MOVE ON.

Step 3
Believe in Yourself

*There were times when I really felt like giving up
. . . I suppose I'm proof that you should always
keep going and believe in yourself.*

KELLY HOLMES, SPEAKING AT THE 'WOMEN
OF THE YEAR' PRESENTATION

Olympic golden girl, Kelly Holmes, was presented with the
outstanding achievement award at the Women of the Year
presentation at the Savoy Hotel, in recognition of the determination and courage she displayed in Athens where she
won two gold medals in 2004. Kelly's career has been
plagued by injury but she has dreamt of the Olympics since
she was twelve and her sheer grit and self-belief won through
for her in the end.

In 1996 she suffered a hairline fracture and had to walk
across the 1,500m finish line, after which she threw away her
spikes in utter disappointment and frustration. At that time
Kelly says that she 'hated the sport . . . I hated everything
about it.' The next year at the World Championships, she
tore her Achilles tendon so badly that she was told she might
never run again. Then in Sydney where she was in with a
chance for Gold, she caught a virus and all her hopes were
dashed once more. At this stage many would have given up
but Kelly has this to say, 'I guess I am a fighter . . . It was

tough thinking, "It's now or never." Athens was my last chance to achieve my dream.' Of course the rest is history!

Believe the best about yourself

Persistence, determination, focus and commitment are the talents that we need when facing adversity in any form. These powerful inner strengths are available to all of us as long as we can believe in ourselves. But as soon as we indulge in self-doubt these magic talents disappear; we lose sight of our goal and we lose the will to follow through for ourselves. Winners in life (as in sport) are those who never give up, whatever the challenges. Winning a race might mean being the best and coming first, but having a winning mentality is about being the best you can be, whatever the circumstances.

Having the confidence to keep on keeping on is all about having unshakeable self-belief; in fact our self-confidence rises and falls in direct proportion to our self-belief.

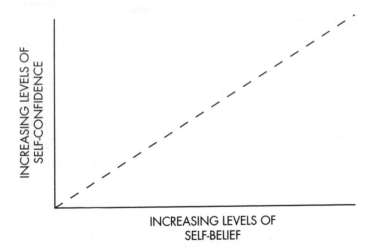

THE RELATIONSHIP BETWEEN
SELF-CONFIDENCE AND SELF-BELIEF

What do you believe to be true about yourself? Are you dynamic, kind and creative or are you lazy, useless and no-good? We run with a mixed bag of beliefs: on a good day believing the best about ourselves and on a more challenging day believing the worst. Our beliefs change, they aren't etched in stone. Remember a recent time when you were buzzing with self-confidence; what did you believe about yourself? But where does that strong self-belief go to at a time when you are feeling less than your best? What is your self-image like when the going is not so good?

The most fabulous and wonderful news is that: *Your beliefs about yourself are not necessarily true; they are not facts, they are only what you are **choosing** to believe.* This vital point means that your negative self-beliefs can be changed so that you *can* feel confident and amazing; you have only to decide to believe the best about yourself.

Try the following questionnaire and discover exactly what you do believe to be true about yourself.

EXERCISE:

Check your self-image
Stage 1

What are you really like? Look at the following words. Read through this list putting the words *I am* before each word and score as follows:

0 almost never
1 sometimes
2 often
3 almost always

tolerant	articulate	interesting	sensitive
depressed	worthless	lovable	indecisive
adventurous	kind	shy	happy
bossy	negative	lazy	protective
cynical	trustworthy	unemotional	passive
intelligent	supportive	amusing	optimistic
irritable	worthy	joyful	overbearing
self-conscious	proud	critical	upbeat
free	caring	predictable	demanding
stupid	self-aware	foolish	capable
flexible	temperamental	fearful	helpless
creative	boring	controlled	intuitive
embarrassed	reflective	guilty	spontaneous

Stage 2

Look at where you scored 3. What do you think that you are almost always?

. . . .

These characteristics are part of your self-image. Now consider the ways in which these features of your personality affect your levels of confidence.

. . . .

For example, if you think that you are almost always *helpless*, then your victim-like status will probably attract negative outcomes and poor relationships. However if you consider that you are almost always *upbeat* then you will have a more optimistic and attractive image that will draw exciting new opportunities and positive people into your orbit. The question to ask yourself is, *which of these characteristics increase my self-confidence and wellbeing and which do not?*
Which, if any, of these characteristics would you like to change?

. . . .

Stage 3

Now look at where you scored 0. What do you believe that you are almost never?

. . . .

Your self-image does not include these features. Does the apparent lack of these qualities affect your self-confidence in any way?

. . . .

For example, if you scored 0 for *indecisive* then this would have a very positive effect on your confidence whereas if you are almost never *self-aware* you would be lacking the reflective quality needed to increase your positive self-belief.

Which, if any, of your 'almost never' characteristics would you like to change?

. . . .

Stage 4

List six adjectives that you think describe you best; you can use the words from the list or any of your own.

. . . .

From this thumbnail sketch choose the statement that you think is most significant. This is your **core belief** about yourself and it underpins and helps to create all aspects of your self-image.

My core belief is that I am . . . .

What does this statement reveal to you? Is your core belief positively affirming or is it self-critical? In other words does it encourage high or low self-confidence?

Stage 5

Now stop and think about all your positive qualities. Imagine that you are 'selling' yourself; what are your unique selling points? Or, if that's too hard just imagine that you are someone else who is looking at you: what great things can you see? If you need some encouragement try completing the following:

I love the way I can . . . .
I am proud of myself for . . . .
I feel at my very best when I am . . . .
My skills and strengths are . . . .
I had the time of my life when I . . . .

How do these great qualities of yours relate to your self-confidence? If you are feeling shy about saying positive things about yourself, consider the implications of this. Why not really let go here and show off for all you are worth? How amazing can you allow yourself to be? The greatest obstacle to total confidence is always found within; decide to overcome your own negative self-beliefs and *let confidence into all aspects your life.*

Your self-image review

By now you will have an idea of

- The sort of person that you think you are
- The self-beliefs that enhance your self-image and confidence
- The self-beliefs that diminish your self-image and confidence
- The new positive qualities that you would like to incorporate in your self-image.

Your self-image exactly reflects your levels of self-belief, which in turn affect your levels of confidence. You know that your beliefs can be changed so why not set to it? There is nothing to lose and all to gain!

INSTANT BOOST

LIFT YOURSELF UP

WE LEARNED OUR BELIEFS ABOUT OURSELVES WHEN WE WERE VERY YOUNG. AS BABIES AND SMALL CHILDREN WE UNQUESTIONINGLY ABSORBED AND BELIEVED ALL THE MESSAGES THAT WERE RELAYED IN OUR ENVIRONMENT. THESE MIGHT HAVE BEEN SPOKEN MESSAGES THAT CRITICISED OR APPRECIATED US, OR THEY MIGHT HAVE BEEN MORE SUBTLE THOUGHT AND BEHAVIOUR PATTERNS THAT INFLUENCED OUR HOME LIFE.

- AS SOON AS YOU UNEARTH A BELIEF THAT LEADS TO NEGATIVE FEELINGS AND LOW SELF-WORTH JUST **LET IT GO!**
- DON'T INDULGE IN THE PAST, JUST RECOGNISE WHAT YOU NEED TO KNOW AND THEN MOVE ON.
- CREATE NEW POSITIVE BELIEFS THAT OVERWHELM AND OVERCOME THE OLD NEGATIVE BELIEFS.
- STOP GRINDING YOURSELF DOWN AND START TO LIFT YOURSELF UP!

Feeling good enough to love life

You are unique and only you can know whatever it is that makes you leap out of bed in the morning full of motivation and go! Or maybe it has been too long a time since you have felt like this.

Here we are, with the gift of this one life, and we can make a fabulous go of it or not. Why would any of us decide to give up on ourselves and let our days drift by without meaning and purpose? This world-weariness and languor usually stem from a low-level but constant buzz of internal mental noise that keeps affirming that we are not good enough! You might not even be conscious of this constant negative self-talk but, believe me, we are all indulging in it. So take this chance to investigate your self-beliefs to see exactly where they are leading you.

You are good enough to do and to be anything you wish. Comparison shopping will knock your confidence to the ground so remind yourself again that you are a one-off, a true original and that this is your great strength. Feelings of not being good enough always stem from a belief that we are competing in a personal race with others who are 'more perfect' than we can ever be.

This is a sticking point for so many of my clients. They can name their goal and even tell me the steps that they need to take but then they often hesitate. To believe in yourself enough to go for your goals means that you are absolutely ready to take the necessary action; you can create an action plan and then you can activate it! But you can only do this if you know that you deserve the best and that you truly are good enough *just the way you are*. It is an incredible paradox that you can only change yourself once you can accept yourself (warts and all). Whenever you are spending time trying to be good enough for something or someone you are affirming that you don't deserve to achieve your goals *just yet* and that you can only go for what you want when you are more perfect than you are. And of course that day can never come.

Never let yourself down

What is 'good enough' for one person is not for another. We can never compare our feelings of self-worth; one woman's confidence maker is another's confidence breaker. The two women in question here are Julie Walters and Sharon Osbourne, two divas of the media world airing their views on cosmetic surgery.

Julie Walters says, 'There's something in me that would always say no to a face-lift. I would feel as if I had let myself down and said I'm not good enough.' In this case the decision not to have cosmetic surgery is a mark of inner confidence for Ms Walters.

On the other hand, Sharon Osbourne has positively flaunted her £120,000 worth of body and face altering surgery, it has obviously increased her self-confidence and she says, 'It was worth every penny.'

It is important that we never do anything that leaves us feeling that we have let ourselves down in any way. Self-confidence depends upon our feelings of self-respect and if we are not true to ourselves then we can never feel confident. The next time you are faced with a difficult decision you could try asking yourself this question: What is the very best that I can do for myself in this situation? And then do it! Be true to yourself and it will lead to inner strength and self-belief.

Believe in yourself and others will believe in you

It's amazing how we seem to attract the very energy that we radiate. Isn't it true that when we are feeling positive and bursting with optimism we seem to have more meaningful relationships with just about everybody in our life?

Self-confidence is not just an inner feeling; it actually shows on the outside, in your smile, your walk, your posture, your words, your actions and even in your aura. When you are high in self-belief you carry that high-octane charismatic energy with you and this draws positive attention and interest from others and keeps you in the cycle of success.

However, if we are self-doubting and unsure the very opposite happens: we carry self-critical energy that shows in our body language, speech and conduct. If we are low in self-belief our energy will tend to bring out the negative in others: if we look and act like a victim then we will find it hard to make friends. When we are in this negative cycle we expect the worst from ourself and from others, and so this is what we get! This self-fulfilling prophecy leads to very poor relationships as we start to let others ignore us or treat us badly because we think that this is all that we deserve.

Helena's story

Helena, 24, is a fashion journalist who moved to London after completing her postgraduate course in journalism at Cardiff University. Helena had secured a brilliant job on a glossy magazine but the move had made her miserable because she had left a great gang of friends in Cardiff. At first she went back every weekend but this started to make her even more fed up and confused and it was at this time that she came for coaching.

Helena said that she loved her new job but felt totally isolated at work and in the house that she shared with three other professional girls. 'In Cardiff I know so many people and I love the place, but the great job is here in London. All the people I meet at work are nice enough and the girls in the house are OK though I don't see much of them. I'm beginning to feel like nobody likes me and it's really getting to me. I wonder why I'm not making friends and I think that perhaps I just seem so boring that others can't be bothered with me. I keep wondering whether to chuck the job in and go back to Wales as I'm so unhappy.'

Helena told me that she had always had difficulty making

friends even when she was a little girl and she remembers being excluded and bullied in the playground at primary school. 'I never felt quite as good as the others and so I was always so grateful when they included me. Thinking back now I realise that even as I got older some of my school friends treated me quite badly and I always felt on the fringe of the social scene. When I went to Cardiff four years ago I fell in with a few good people and for the first time I felt that I had got the hang of being a good friend. But now I'm back feeling isolated again and I can't stand it.'

I asked Helena if she had made any overtures to anyone at work but she said that she hadn't because she thought that they wouldn't be interested in her. She had become locked in an old pattern from her childhood and needed to break free of this feeling of 'not being good enough'. I suggested that she started a yoga class that was running locally as this seemed a good way to help her unwind and relax as well as increasing her chances of meeting new people. I also felt that her self-image could do with a polish and so Helena completed the self-image exercise on page 48.

Two weeks later and Helena was a different girl. She had been out for a drink with someone from the yoga class and that had given her the confidence to open up to the girls who shared her house. In fact she told them that she was having coaching with me and this started a fascinating discussion.

Helena was shocked by the results of the self-image exercise and realised just how negative she felt about herself. She said, 'No wonder people aren't rushing to be friends with me when I am acting like such a victim; if I can't believe that I am worth knowing why should anyone else believe it?' After this realisation Helena decided to take the initiative at home and at work. She cooked a meal for her housemates and invited three girls from work and it was a great success. Helena said, 'I can't believe that I just sat around feeling sorry for myself waiting for someone to like me. If I want to make friends I need to get out there and show a bit of spirit. Things are already taking off and I am feeling so much more confident. I have never previously considered the way that our self-belief affects the way that others see us. I'm really pleased to have discovered a way to feel more confident about myself at a deep level.'

INSTANT BOOST

FACE YOUR CHALLENGE

LOOK AT ANY CHALLENGE YOU ARE FACING RIGHT NOW. TAKE YOUR HEAD RIGHT OUT OF THE SAND AND LOOK THE ISSUE IN THE EYE.

SPECIFY THE PROBLEM; NAME THE CONCERNS AND TAKE A CLEAR LOOK AT WHAT CAN BE DONE.

- SAY WHAT NEEDS TO BE DONE OUT LOUD: *I NEED TO* . . .
- DECIDE WHEN YOU WILL TAKE THE FIRST STEP TOWARDS YOUR OUTCOME.
- TAKE THE FIRST STEP.
- THIS WILL NATURALLY LEAD TO THE NEXT STEP; YOU ARE ON YOUR WAY!

The most satisfying thing in the world

When Michelle McManus appeared on the TV show *Pop Idol* she caused a sensation on screen, in the papers and even amongst some MPs. Of course she has a fabulous voice but it was her obvious body confidence that created such a stir. The media struggled to accept that Michelle could be happy in her own skin (because she didn't conform to the pop diva stereotype) and Pete Waterman's negative comments about her weight were even condemned in the House of Commons. Michelle always knew that her weight would be an issue but that didn't stop her going for her dream; she says, 'I didn't stop to think, "Oh what will people say about me – I'm too big."'

Michelle is a girl who values herself and her talents and will not let anyone else's opinion stand in her way. In an interview with *Cosmopolitan* she said, 'Being on *Pop Idol* was never about my weight. I never said, "Please vote for me because I'm fat, I'm so hard done by." I wanted people to vote for me if they liked my voice.' Michelle is a wonderful demonstration of how much can be achieved when we steadfastly refuse to let our self-belief be undermined by anybody else. If you think that you need to change yourself in any way before you can be allowed to go for your goals, just stop and think again. Take strength from Michelle's example and these final words from her: 'You're you and you have to love yourself for who you are. It might sound cheesy, but it's the most satisfying thing in the world to be happy and comfortable with yourself.'

- Think about your biggest goals. Are you working towards achieving them or do they just feel like fanciful dreams?

- If they feel a long way from being realised just spend a few moments considering why this is.
- Name the obstacles in your path.
- Now what would you need to believe about yourself in order to overcome these difficulties?
- Write a list of these new self-beliefs.
- Now begin to believe them!

INNER REFLECTION

RELAX AND LET GO

FIND A COMFORTABLE POSITION, EITHER SITTING OR LYING DOWN AND CLOSE YOUR EYES.

- TAKE A DEEP BREATH, AND AS YOU EXHALE LET ALL YOUR STRESSES AND STRAINS JUST FADE AWAY AWAY.
- CONCENTRATE ON YOUR BREATH AND BECOME AWARE OF THE RHYTHM OF YOUR BREATHING.
- AS YOU INHALE, IMAGINE THAT YOU ARE BEING FILLED WITH PEACE AND CALM.
- AND AS YOU EXHALE, VISUALISE THAT YOU ARE LETTING GO OF ALL THE TENSION IN YOUR BODY.
- FOLLOW YOUR BREATHING, INHALING PEACE AND EXHALING PHYSICAL TENSION.

SOME PEOPLE FIND IT EASIER TO FOCUS ON THEIR BREATHING BY SAYING TO THEMSELVES *FILLING WITH PEACE* AS THEY INHALE, AND SAYING *LETTING GO OF TENSION* AS THE EXHALE. OTHERS LIKE TO IMAGINE THEMSELVES BREATHING IN A BEAUTIFUL PINK LIGHT AND

RELEASING ALL IMPURITIES AS THEY BREATHE OUT. TRY ANY VERSION OF THIS MEDITATION AND SEE WHAT SUITS YOU BEST.

YOU CAN USE THIS SIMPLE BREATHING TECHNIQUE AT ANY TIME, IT IS BRILLIANTLY EFFECTIVE AND NO ONE CAN TELL THAT YOU ARE DOING IT. IT'S PARTICULARLY USEFUL WHEN YOU FEEL YOURSELF BECOMING ANXIOUS OR ANGRY; IT GIVES YOU THE CALM SPACE YOU NEED JUST TO COOL DOWN AND GET THINGS IN PERSPECTIVE.

USE IT WHENEVER YOU FEEL THE NEED TO CENTRE YOUR ENERGY AND LET GO OF ANXIETY; JUST ALLOW YOURSELF TO RELAX AND LET GO. THE MORE YOU PRACTISE THIS TECHNIQUE THE MORE EFFECTIVE IT BECOMES.

Step 4
Get Going

Before I turn 67 – next March – I would like to have a lot of sex with a man I like. If you want to talk first, Trollope works for me.

JANE JUSKA

Life coaching lays it on the line: you can change any aspect of your life if you so wish, but to do this you must take total responsibility for the ways that you think, feel and act. You are reading this book because you are ready to change and you know that a cynical, negative, fearful or blaming approach will never bring you the confidence you seek. We only attract success when we are ready to step out of our comfort zone and feel the fear and then do it anyway! Winners and achievers are risk-takers; they are ready to do things a little differently, they are not afraid of making mistakes and they know what they want and are willing to do whatever it takes to get it. Confidence comes to those who are ready to come out of the closet and name their goal and then go for it.

Fifteen years ago I was at a residential counselling course in a Torquay hotel. The training weekend was at an end and the participants were asked what they had got from the course. When it came to my turn I found myself saying that I had decided to write a self-help book. I certainly wasn't consciously aware of having made this decision so it came as much as a surprise to me as to everyone else. As I drove back home I felt the first stirrings of self-doubt: why had I said that I'd write a book; why did I tell all those people; what if it didn't happen? My fears were all about not coming through and looking a fool but as I drove it became clear that *I didn't care* about any of these things because *I cared so much more* about achieving my goal. After that I realised that telling everybody had been a great idea because now I would have to do it. At the time we were living in Gorran Haven, a tiny fishing village close to St Austell in Cornwall. It's the sort of place where everyone knows what you are doing almost before you have done it! So I carried on with this plan of telling people about my book and by the end of the week villagers were asking me what it was to be called, what it was about etc., etc., and by then of course, there really was no going back!

I'm telling you this because I think coming out and naming my goal to so many people proved to be a winning technique for me and it's one I have since used again and again. When you positively affirm that you will do something and you care more about the outcome than the possibility of failure you are certain to be successful. How can you fail when you back your dreams? What does it matter if things don't go exactly the way you had envisaged? You will always feel like a winner when you are reaching for your very best as this approach always brings bucket loads of confidence; you cannot possibly fail to feel fabulous about yourself.

Once you are clear about what you want it's time to get going on what it will take to achieve it. And whatever you want, whether it's fame and fortune, a new job, to make sense of the past, a better relationship, to write a book or even to have a lot of sex, you will only achieve it when you focus single-mindedly on your goal.

The quotation at the beginning of this chapter is actually an ad placed in *The New York Review of Books* by Jane Juska, a retired teacher aged 67, who reads Trollope and admires good prose. Having not had sex for 40 years Jane decides that it's time for her to catch up on possible missed pleasures. After placing the ad she embarked on the dating game with gusto and eventually wrote the best-selling book, *A Round-Heeled Woman: My Late Life Adventures in Sex and Romance.*

Hats off to Ms Juska for her audacity and sheer daring even though we might not share the same goal. The point, surely, is that whenever we want something new to happen we have to act in new ways: that brilliant stunning outcome will stay in the realms of fantasy until you are ready to put yourself out there and *get going and make it happen.*

GO-GETTERS

INSTANT BOOST

YOU CAN DO IT

WHEN YOU BELIEVE THAT YOU CAN DO IT, YOU CAN, AND WHEN YOU DON'T BELIEVE YOU CAN DO IT, YOU CAN'T; IT'S AS SIMPLE AS THIS. SO GET BELIEVING!

MAKE A LIST OF ALL YOUR PAST ACHIEVEMENTS, NOT FORGETTING YOUR CHILDHOOD TRIUMPHS. CAN YOU REMEMBER LEARNING TO RIDE A BIKE; SWIMMING A WIDTH; JOINING THE BROWNIES; YOUR FIRST LOVE AFFAIR; PASSING YOUR DRIVING TEST; GETTING YOUR FIRST JOB? ENJOY THIS PROCESS OF HIGHLIGHTING YOUR SUCCESSES.

KEEP ADDING TO THIS LIST WHENEVER YOU REMEMBER SOMETHING NEW AND AS THE DAYS PASS AND YOUR LIST GROWS ALLOW YOURSELF SEVERAL PATS ON THE BACK.

CAN YOU SEE HOW COURAGEOUS YOU ARE? YOU ARE A RISK-TAKER AND A GO-GETTER. LOOK AT HOW YOU MUCH YOU HAVE ALREADY ACHIEVED.

YOU SEE, YOU REALLY ARE A 'CAN-DO' SORT OF PERSON. NEXT TIME YOU FIND YOURSELF DOUBTING IF YOU CAN DO IT (WHATEVER IT IS) TAKE ANOTHER LOOK AT THIS GROWING LIST. YOU HAVE GOT EXACTLY WHAT IT TAKES TO DO WHATEVER YOU NEED TO DO; START TO BELIEVE THIS.

But what will other people think?

We can imagine that Jane Juska's raunchy go-getting style might have raised a few eyebrows amongst her circle of friends and acquaintances; but hey, an assertive girl must care more about her goal than about what others might think.

Jenny Eclair, comedienne and broadcaster, says, 'I've elbowed myself to where I am in my career, like a woman fighting for bargains at a jumble sale, so I really shouldn't be surprised that there are people who find me ghastly, over-loud and simply much too much.' I love her analogy because it beautifully reminds us of that feeling of really wanting something and being prepared to go to the limit for it. And this is how strongly you must feel about your goal; unless you passionately desire your outcome you will not be able to stretch yourself to the limits that will be necessary to achieve it.

Winning sportspeople, great actors, wonderful artists, in fact anyone who gains our respect and admiration does so because we know that they have worked for their success; talent alone is never enough but talent and focus are a winning combination every time. To be focused means being prepared to override our feelings of self-doubt, fear of failure and worry about what other people might think of us. We can never please all of the people all of the time and when we step outside our usual patterns of activity and start to go for something fresh, new and exciting there may well be ripples of unease amongst our friends and loved ones. Dynamic go-getting energy can sometimes be very confronting; particularly to those who are feeling stuck themselves. So if your great plans meet with negativity be prepared to *take no notice;* if someone laughs at you or doubts your ability just *don't let it get to you.* If this goal is really important to you and you have the focus and commitment to see it through then what other people think is of no consequence!

About ten years ago when I was running motivational courses for the Employment Service in Cornwall, I met Phil who was then 28 and had been out of work for six months. He was an angry and depressed young man who had left school at 16 with no exam passes and over the years he had worked in various low-paid and unrewarding summer jobs in the tourist industry and signed on in the winter months. Phil was called to attend one of my courses because he had been unemployed for six months. These courses ran for a month and attendance was compulsory or benefit was stopped, so you can easily see why the participants were often less than happy to be there. Running these courses was the most challenging work that I have ever done but it was also incredibly stimulating and at times utterly rewarding; I learned a lot from long-term unemployed people about what it takes to overcome low self-esteem.

Phil's story

Phil started off on the wrong foot on the first day and he looked set to confront me every step of the way for the next four weeks. He was an intelligent man who carried a chip on his shoulder about those who worked in a professional capacity and had 'qualifications'; he was very low in confidence and self-respect and his anger masked these feelings. His social scene revolved around the local pub and his mates were similarly unmotivated and fed-up and they considered it 'cool' to laugh at anyone who was trying to improve their own situation.

But as the group worked through the various skills and

strength analyses, and discussed their future goals, Phil slowly began to change. One morning I arrived late only to discover that the group was involved in writing personal action plans and that Phil was guiding them. One of the course members had difficulty writing and Phil was sitting next to him to help him. And this was Phil's turning point; he had stepped in to help me out and found something amazing within himself. From that day he never looked back, he stopped arguing with me about how hopeless his prospects were and how he could never change his situation and turned his energy around to help himself. The most difficult part of this process was when his so-called mates starting to laugh at his attempts to move on and he and I spent a long time discussing the implications of this. Eventually he realised that if he was going to change his circumstances he would have to leave his moaning mates behind and this he did. At the end of the month he had found a job as a teaching assistant at the local primary school and declared that his long-term goal was to train to be a teacher himself.

Last year when I went back to Cornwall I discovered that he had indeed reached his goal and was teaching in a primary school in Devon. Once Phil had decided that he cared more about his future than what his mates down the pub thought, he stepped out of a cycle of defeat and straight into a success cycle. Look out for people who support failure rather than achievement and stay away from them. And when someone criticises you or laughs at you, just remember that this says much more about them than it does about you.

- *Stay away from people who are critical and negative.*
- *Spend time with those who give you positive encouragement.*

- *Ignore anyone who tries to feed your self-doubt, and ask yourself why they would do this.*
- *Stop trying to please others and start to please yourself.*

INNER REFLECTION

APPRECIATE YOUR FAN CLUB

QUIETLY REFLECT ON THOSE PEOPLE WHO ARE YOUR GREATEST FANS. THESE ARE THE ONES WHO ARE ALWAYS TELLING YOU THINGS LIKE 'HAVE A GO', 'YOU CAN DO IT', 'I BELIEVE IN YOU'. SOMETIMES WE SPEND OUR ENERGY TRYING TO PLEASE PEOPLE WHO DO NOT GIVE US THEIR SUPPORT AND WE FORGET ABOUT OUR FAN CLUB.

SPEND A FEW MOMENTS NOW JUST APPRECIATING THOSE WHO APPRECIATE YOU. THESE ARE THE PEOPLE WHO DO YOU THE GREATEST SERVICE AND SEEK THE BEST OUTCOME FOR YOU; THEY WILL NOT BE INTIMIDATED OR THREAT-ENED BY YOUR SUCCESS AND THEY WILL BE THERE FOR YOU EVERY STEP OF THE WAY. SILENTLY ACKNOWLEDGE THEM AND THANK THEM FOR THEIR SUPPORT.

Activating an idea

Imagine this: You are full of anticipation and excitement about a new project; you feel inspired and are full of great plans, but then this first flush of enthusiasm suddenly starts to fade when you get down to the practical details of your scheme. This isn't very hard to imagine, is it? How many times have you felt that initial rush of buoyancy and motivation that accompanies a new creative idea only to experience, a little later, a complete loss of confidence and belief in your project?

Watch a small child at imaginative play and you will see the ultimate in positive focus, belief and motivation; 'make-believe' allows complete creative flexibility and is never challenged by real-life considerations. When my grand-daughter puts her dolls through a hard session at 'school' she is the most bossy, authoritarian teacher in the world, and does she get results! Her self-confidence and assertive skills are a wonder to behold as she creates her own powerful reality in the realm of her imagination. And it's here, in our imagination, that we first conceive of any idea. At this stage it's so easy to believe in our success as we visualise ourselves reaching easily for our goal and living our personal fantasy. The next step requires that we make a realistic action plan so that we can begin to really create our outcome, and it's at this stage that we often come unstuck.

You need to know that we all have unfinished projects lying around under the stairs, in the attic, in a sewing box, in the garage, in our heads . . . The move *from fabulous idea* to *practical application of fabulous idea* takes self-confidence, self-belief, patience, hard work and time! Trust me, those uncompleted schemes of yours were just not fabulous enough to entice you to the finishing line. Go-getters reach their goals because they are passionately and totally in love with them; so check your level of heartfelt commitment before you even begin to think of creating an action plan.

- MAKE A LIST OF ALL YOUR UNFINISHED PROJECTS. I KNOW YOU DON'T WANT TO BUT I PROMISE THAT THIS EXERCISE WILL BE CATHARTIC.

- NOW, BE RUTHLESS AND REALISTIC AND CROSS OFF THOSE THAT YOU KNOW YOU WILL NEVER BE ABLE TO FINISH. DISPOSE OF THEM PHYSICALLY AND MENTALLY. (IF ANY OF THEM ARE LONG-STANDING DIY JOBS THEN YOU MAY HAVE TO PAY SOMEONE ELSE TO DO THEM.)

- TAKE ALL DEBRIS ASSOCIATED WITH THE PROJECTS TO THE TIP; AND WHEN YOU RETURN YOU WILL FEEL BOTH CLEANSED AND VIRTUOUS.

- NOW TAKE A LOOK AT THE REST OF YOUR LIST. PRIORITISE THESE TASKS, BEGINNING WITH THE EASIEST.

- START WORK ON THE ONE AT THE TOP OF THE LIST. YES, JUST DO IT! BEGIN NOW.

- COME CLEAN AND UNCLUTTER YOUR MIND. YOU ARE A PERSON WHO FULFILS COMMITMENTS.

Face to face with the risk

Everything we do involves some sort of action plan; even making dinner requires that we buy the ingredients and have some knowledge of how to cook. We often don't acknowledge the effort and planning that goes into most of our tasks because we just do them naturally, they are part of our habitual routine and they feel easy. But when we decide to make changes we have to move beyond our own particular habits and then we enter uncharted territory: this is a journey into the unknown and we are bound to be uncertain. Face it: the change you seek must challenge you or you would have done it already.

EXERCISE:

The best and the worst that can happen

I often run this exercise in workshops as it is so good at weeding out any unrealistic fears that might be standing in our way.

1 Think of something new that you would like to do or anything that you would like to change or a specific goal that you want to go for.
   My goal is . . . .

2 Now ask yourself what could be the best possible outcome for you.
   The best thing that can happen is . . . .

3 Consider the worst possible outcome.
   The worst thing that can happen is . . . .

4 In what ways, if any, do your fears and anxieties help or hinder you? . . . .
   . . . .

5 Name any fears and anxieties that you would like to overcome. . . . .

What are those fears that are in your way? How realistic are they? Will the sky fall in if you take a stand? If the newly assertive you rocks the boat, then so be it; maybe it's time to start to make waves. And what if others don't like the changes you are planning? Check out these people's motives; remember that true friends will always support your positive development. Balance the benefits of going for your goal against the realisation of your fears; now why not decide to feel those fears and do it anyway?

The realisation of a new and fabulous goal will always feel risky; change is a risky business: *what if I fail, look a fool, they don't like me any more, people think I'm pushy. . .* so what! The very worst that can happen is that you are too afraid to take the risk and have to live with the consequences of your inaction. How can we expect others to treat us with respect if we can't come through for ourselves? Confidence comes to those who are prepared to take a chance, to make that leap of faith and to know that, whatever the consequences, they had the courage to have a go!

When you put your life on hold

- What are you waiting for?
- Why can't you take that leap of faith and say what you really want and then go for it?
- Are you afraid that you are still not *good enough, thin enough, successful enough. . .* to take the lead in your own drama?
- Are you hiding in the wings watching others take the roles that you would dearly love?
- Are you a perfectionist?

Anne Wilson Schaef makes an interesting observation in her book, *Meditations For Women Who Do Too Much:* she says that '. . . we may use perfectionism to keep ourselves from getting anything done. If it has to be done perfectly, why even start? Perfectionism and procrastination go hand in hand, and accomplish nothing.'

Take a look at the following list of types of avoidance behaviours and how we rationalise them; perhaps you will see yourself here.

- **Thinking about what's to be done** and not doing it – this has been called 'armchair contemplation'. We have all done this and it's surprisingly easy to believe that our thinking about doing the paperwork (for example) is actually having an effect on the end result. Sadly this is not the case.
- **Adopting the mañana approach.** You might even believe that you *will* do it tomorrow but it's more than likely that you won't; and so tomorrow never comes.
- **Making other tasks more important** than the one you are putting off. Suddenly the bathroom needs a good clean before you can get down to writing that proposal, applying for a new job or whatever.
- **Pretending that you are doing the task** by making the necessary preparations and then considering that you have done enough for today.
- **Distracting yourself** with coffee breaks, phone calls and other minor pleasures and all the while the task remains untouched.
- **Trying to get 'in the right mood'** by doing other things that feel more pleasurable, and then suddenly the day has slipped by and the job isn't done.
- **Feeling too afraid to be assertive** and pretending that it's better to 'keep the peace'; you will say what you want to say when the right moment arrives, which of course it never does.

- **Masking your fears of failure** by leaving tasks until the very last minute. It might be true that you work best under pressure but it's much more likely that you don't. Of course, if you are a perfectionist you will always have the perfect excuse for yourself if you can never give a project the time it needs.
- **Waiting to feel motivated** enough to get going. But we often have to take that difficult first step before we can feel the motivation we seek. Action is the greatest motivator.
- **Doing too much** and juggling too many plates. This ensures that you never have the time or the energy to get going on the things that are really most important to you; a fabulous excuse when you are afraid to go for your goals.
- **Worrying incessantly** about what you have to do so that you become unable to make clear decisions and create a workable action plan. This is a surefire way to drive yourself into the cycle of defeat.

You might have come up with other avoidance strategies; we all have our unique ways to put things off. But the most important issue here is not to criticise yourself for your apparent weak will and slackness, but rather to understand the way that you operate. Recognise your strategies and then the next time they emerge you will become aware of what you are doing and what you need to do to change. Self-awareness is the precursor for change; we cannot move on in any way if we aren't conscious of where we have come from and where we want to go.

For example, a client who was two stone overweight recognised that she was most likely to dive into the Häagen-

Dazs tub when she was feeling fearful of socialising. She found herself in a repeating cycle where friends asked her out and she was too terrified to go (because she wasn't thin enough, pretty enough, good enough . . . etc.) and so spent the evening alone with ice-cream and chocolate biscuits. Once she became aware of her fear she felt able to challenge it. She talked about the way that she 'stuffed' her feelings by stuffing herself with sugary delights and how she really hated doing this. After this realisation she decided to accept the next social invitation, however terrified she felt. Of course she had a great time and now goes out a few nights a week. And when she stays in she is no longer compelled to overeat, in fact she has been going to Weight Watchers and is close to her target weight.

The moral of this story is, don't miss out on your life by spending your days putting things off; life is too short to wait until your feel *perfect enough.*

10 Ways to get going

1 **Stop trying to be perfect.** This is a trap that will prevent you moving forward and reaching your potential. Recognise that perfectionism is a myth and that it is standing in your way.

2 **Take the first step towards a short-term goal.** Action is such a brilliant motivator and it gives you all the confidence you need to take the next few steps.

3 **Listen to the excuses you make.** Get to know yourself and the strategies you use to stop yourself going for your goals. And then stop making those excuses!

4 **Write a to-do list.** Now do the most important thing on your list; how fabulous do you feel?

5 **Concentrate on the rewards of getting going.** Imagine that the task is completed and bask in that great glow of accomplishment. Let this feeling be the carrot that gets you going.

6 **Believe in yourself and know that you cannot fail.** When you put yourself forward and give life the best you have got you can never lose, because you will always know that you are a 'can do' and 'will do' person who has tenacity and courage.

7 **Have the confidence to come through for yourself.** There is no one as powerful as the person who is in touch with what she wants and is ready to do whatever she needs to get it. Why would you deserve anything less?

8 **Do one scary thing every day.** Practice facing your fears by doing something that feels slightly risky every day. Go on, speak to that gorgeous man at work; get your hair cut in a new way; try learning a new skill; visit a different restaurant; book a snowboarding holiday. . .

9 **Look in the mirror and promise to get going.** Look yourself in the eyes and make a commitment to yourself. Give yourself the respect you deserve and do whatever you have promised; there is no going back.

10 **Take control of your life.** Only you can activate the changes you seek, decide to go for it now. Just do it!

INNER REFLECTION

WHEN THE DANDELION HAS YOUR SMILE

ZEN MASTER AND PEACE ACTIVIST THICH NHAT HANH TALKS ABOUT THE TRUE VALUE OF OUR SMILE AND AWARENESS IN HIS WONDERFUL BOOK *PEACE IS EVERY STEP*:

'OUR SMILE WILL BRING HAPPINESS TO US AND TO THOSE AROUND US. EVEN IF WE SPEND A LOT OF MONEY ON GIFTS FOR EVERYONE IN OUR FAMILY, NOTHING WE BUY COULD GIVE THEM AS MUCH HAPPINESS AS THE GIFT OF OUR AWARENESS, OUR SMILE. AND THIS PRECIOUS GIFT COSTS NOTHING.

'AT THE END OF A RETREAT IN CALIFORNIA, A FRIEND WROTE THIS POEM:

> *I HAVE LOST MY SMILE,*
> *BUT DON'T WORRY.*
> *THE DANDELION HAS IT.*

'IF YOU HAVE LOST YOUR SMILE AND YET ARE STILL CAPABLE OF SEEING THAT A DANDELION IS KEEPING IT FOR YOU, THE SITUATION IS NOT TOO BAD.'

- WHEN DARK CLOUDS PASS OVER YOUR LIFE AND YOU LOSE YOUR SENSE OF HUMOUR, YOU ONLY NEED TO BECOME AWARE THAT YOU ARE NOT ISOLATED IN YOUR SADNESS.
- OPEN UP TO THE SUPPORT THAT IS ALL AROUND YOU AND ALSO WITHIN YOU.

- NEXT TIME YOU LOSE YOUR SMILE, REMEMBER THAT IT IS NOT LOST FOREVER. BECOME AWARE THAT YOUR SMILE IS JUST BEING 'LOOKED AFTER' FOR THE TIME BEING AND THAT IT WILL RETURN.
- SAY TO YOURSELF, 'THE DANDELION HAS MY SMILE', AND LET THIS SWEET THOUGHT LIFT YOUR SPIRITS AND HEIGHTEN YOUR AWARENESS: YOU ARE NEVER ALONE IN YOUR SADNESS.

Step 5
Love Your Life

One of the lies we tell ourselves is that if we do not let ourselves love completely, then we will be less hurt. Loving in a halfhearted manner, pursuing our dreams in a halfhearted manner, we are divided against ourselves. We do ourselves the indignity of not taking ourselves seriously, and we do our creative projects the serious injustice of refusing to visualise them with clarity. Because clarity of vision is a trigger to manifestation, our self-protective desire to hedge our bets can result in our projects not coming to fruition.

JULIA CAMERON

It's always so easy to see when others have their heads stuck in the sand, isn't it? As soon as we start to act like ostriches we lose sight of what we are doing (because our heads are of course stuck in that proverbial sand); so when we ourselves first go into denial we are unaware that we are doing so. The first clues come fairly quickly – we feel: fed-up; ill at ease; depressed; low in energy; frustrated; lacking in confidence; muddled; irritated; victimised . . . to name just a few unpleasant symptoms.

Alongside these feelings we might recognise that our behaviour is reactive rather than proactive; in other words we are responding to the overtures of others rather than stepping out there and creating our own experiences. We might be telling ourselves that we are only 'hedging our bets' and 'keeping our options open', and indeed these are tactics that *are* useful when we are assessing possibilities. But as soon as we 'know' what it is that we want, then we must come forward and declare our wishes to ourselves. This means recognising our heart's desire (whatever we would love to do or be) and then setting about achieving it. If we fail to do this then we become what Julia Cameron describes as 'divided against ourselves' and this causes us many problems.

Halfhearted commitment and behaviour is exactly that; it doesn't engage our whole heart, we are not putting all our love into our life. And if we cannot bring love and clarity to our daily experiences then we will stay in that cycle of defeat. Love is the key that allows us to open up to our true feelings and our wonderful potential and it places us firmly into the positive cycle of success. Love reveals itself in trust, belief and faith in ourselves and the process of life. Self-belief demonstrates itself in confident, enthusiastic and motivated behaviour (I know what I want and I can rise to any challenge). When we choose to love our lives rather than just to live our lives we embrace an expansive awareness; our hearts and minds are open and we are able to feel compassion for ourselves and others.

INSTANT BOOST

OPEN UP YOUR HEART

WE ALL KNOW WHAT IT'S LIKE WHEN OUR HEART FEELS CLOSED AND SHRIVELLED AND WE ARE UNABLE TO APPRECIATE OUR FABULOUS LIFE. TRY THESE HEART-OPENING TECHNIQUES:

- THINK OF SOMEONE YOU CARE ABOUT AND THEN LET THEM KNOW JUST HOW VERY MUCH THEY MEAN TO YOU. SEND AN EMAIL, MAKE A PHONE CALL, WRITE A CARD, SHARE A HUG . . . GIVE YOUR LOVE AND YOU WILL FEEL BRILLIANT.
- HAVE A GRATITUDE SESSION. START LOOKING FOR THINGS TO BE GRATEFUL FOR: THE FIRST TINY SNOW-DROP, THE LAUGHTER OF A CHILD, AN ACT OF KINDNESS . . . GO OUT AND LOOK FOR BEAUTY AND YOU WILL FEEL YOUR HEARTSTRINGS TUGGING.
- GET CREATIVE AND FEEL YOURSELF GETTING INTO THAT HARMONIOUS FLOW OF ENERGY. MAKE A CAKE, PICK SOME FLOWERS, CHANGE A ROOM AROUND, LIGHT CANDLES AT THE DINNER TABLE. FOCUS ALL YOUR ATTENTION ON WHATEVER IT IS YOU DO AND ADMIRE THE RESULTS. YES, YOU DO MAKE A DIFFERENCE; BE GLAD JUST TO BE ALIVE.
- LAUGH AND JUMP FOR JOY. SHOW THE WORLD HOW MUCH YOU LOVE IT, AND IF YOU ARE NOT FEELING UP TO THIS *JUST PRETEND!* JUMP UP AND DOWN SHOUTING 'I LOVE MY LIFE'; FAKE IT UNTIL YOU MAKE IT, AS WE SAY IN LIFE COACHING. GIVE IT A GO, I PROMISE THIS WILL MAKE YOU LAUGH OR CRY (BOTH HEARTFELT EMOTIONS).
- FORGIVE YOURSELF. MORE OF THIS LATER.

The enduring power of love

Two weeks ago (while I was writing this book) my dear mother-in-law Mary Field died at the age of 87. She lived in a small village nestled in the Quantock Hills in Somerset and we held her funeral there.

Mary was an inspiration to all who met her and she was a constant reminder of how to live life to the maximum; she led by example and she taught us how to love and enjoy life. She was a great networker and her death prompted an extraordinary number of people to come forward and speak about their relationship with her. Over the funeral weekend two clear life themes emerged: the sheer exuberance and enthusiasm that she demonstrated in all that she did and the kindness and patience that she showed to all those she met. Mary put love at the centre of her life and because of this her energy was creative and dynamic. She loved music and was an accomplished musician, singer and teacher. When the church bells were broken a few years ago, she began the handbell ringing group which became famous in the area; she played her last 'gig' with them in a local school two weeks before she became ill. She also loved her garden, which she opened to the public every year. Mary was even playing table tennis at the age of 85 and was preparing for her Latin GCSE right up to the day of her stroke. She was always ready to learn something new and approached all her projects with confidence and zest. Everything she did she did with gusto, no half measures only total commitment. I hope that I can continue her tradition in some small way.

Since her death I am noticing and valuing my life even more. I feel duty bound to honour her shining example by stepping forward rather than shrinking back in the face of a potential challenge. When in doubt I have started to say to myself, 'What would Mary do?' and I can feel her urging me on, saying, 'Go on, you can do it.'

Mary's greatest legacy to her family and to all those who knew her was to remind us of the enduring power of love. A lover of life engages in the creative flow and is inspired to reach for their very best and surely this is the greatest skill of all. When we can let our lives become an exciting adventure we overcome our inhibitions and doubts with our sheer drive and passion. When you love your life it will love you back.

Loving your life means ...

- Reaching for your best at all times.
- Knowing that everything changes and that dark times will pass.
- Having faith in yourself and other people.
- Looking for the fun and joy in life and finding a way to share these things with others.
- Going with the creative flow and making something of your life.
- Believing in your unique skills and using them.
- Never forgetting that life is precious.
- Seeing the good and the positive in all things.
- Living life to the full.
- Understanding that there is always something new and exciting to learn.
- Encouraging and inspiring others along the way.
- Being able to open your heart, every day.
- Letting yourself off the hook.

Taking the path with heart

Jack Kornfield is trained in clinical psychology and is also a Buddhist monk. In his acclaimed book, *A Path with Heart,* he says, 'We must make certain that our path is connected to our heart . . . When we ask, "Am I following a path with heart?" we discover that no one can define for us exactly what our path should be . . . If we are still and listen deeply, even for a moment, we will know if we are following a path with heart.'

We all have days when we just don't feel at our best and on such a day it is hard to feel overflowing with love for the universe and its inhabitants. But when we are feeling challenged by life we still have to make important choices and decisions. There are times when we act out of fear instead of love: maybe we treat someone badly and cause them pain or are unable to be true to our feelings or just get sidetracked by doubt so that we can't fulfil our commitments. When this happens we find that we have left our heart path and are drifting into a state of apathy, depression, negativity and lack of confidence.

EXERCISE:

Is your heart in it?

1 Whenever you feel less than your best just stop for a moment and check the true nature of your present path.

On a path with heart:
- You feel great.
- Relationships are supportive.
- You are motivated and positive.

- There is a feeling of 'connectedness' as if you are 'going with the flow'.
- There is a sense of being in the right place at the right time.

2 Take any difficult area of your life and check for the above points.

For example, if you are not feeling motivated and positive at work even though your colleagues are supportive then something is obviously wrong. Your heart is not in your career choice. So why are you still in this job? Fear of change? Lack of self-confidence? Apathy? You need to question your behaviour and decide to be true to yourself.

3 Apply this procedure to any area of your life where you are feeling unhappy – and remember: if your heart is not in it, your life will not feel worth living.

4 Ask yourself some searching questions. Challenge your own behaviour and actions: why are you being untrue to yourself? Seek some answers; take courage. Take the path with heart.

Follow your dream

Even if you haven't read Paulo Coelho's *The Alchemist* you will most probably have heard of it. It is the magical story of Santiago, an Andalusian shepherd boy who dreams of travelling the world in search of a treasure as fabulous as any ever found. And so he leaves his home in Spain and journeys to the Egyptian desert, following a path of omens to his destiny. Eventually he meets an alchemist who inspires Santiago to stay true to his dreams.

INSTANT BOOST

YOUR LOVE LIST

RELAX AND LET GO OF ALL PREOCCUPATIONS.

YOU MIGHT LIKE TO LISTEN TO A FAVOURITE PIECE OF MUSIC AS YOU TURN YOUR ATTENTION TO THE SIMPLE THINGS IN YOUR LIFE THAT YOU MOST LOVE AND APPRECIATE.

LET YOUR MIND WANDER AS YOU PICK OUT AT LEAST 40 ITEMS THAT YOU *ABSOLUTELY LOVE!* MAKE A LIST OF THEM AND BE AS SPECIFIC AND DETAILED AS YOU CAN SO THAT YOU CAPTURE THEIR VERY ESSENCE.

SOME EXAMPLES FROM CLIENTS ARE:
- THE SMELL OF ORANGES
- MAKING FOOTPRINTS ON FRESHLY FALLEN SNOW
- LYING IN THE SUN
- THE SOUND OF CHURCH BELLS
- THE SCENT OF ROSES
- GREAT AUNT SUSAN'S TREACLE TART
- MY BABY GODDAUGHTER'S GURGLING LAUGH
- SINGING CHRISTMAS CAROLS
- SPENDING TIME WITH MY BEST FRIEND
- MY SISTER JEAN'S DRAWINGS
- LOOKING AT PHOTOS OF MY FAMILY WHEN THEY WERE YOUNG
- THE DIMPLES ON MY BABY'S BOTTOM
- THE SCENT OF NEW-MOWN HAY
- READING A BOOK IN BED

One night as they look up at a moonless sky Santiago confides to the alchemist that he is terrified of following his heart's desire. He says, 'My heart is afraid that it will have to suffer.' And the alchemist says, 'Tell your heart that the fear of suffering is worse than the suffering itself . . . no heart has ever suffered when it goes in search of its dreams, because every second of the search is a second's encounter with God and eternity.'

Once we name a dream and start to visualise it coming true we will encounter personal resistance, which is quite natural. There is so much to fear: the unknown, the obstacles along the way, the possibility of defeat and disappointment, our feelings of not deserving good fortune . . . and so they go on, a litany of excuses to keep us from going for our most exciting goals. It is at this point that we can do ourselves the serious injustice of refusing to get clear about the steps we need to take. How often have you backed away from one of your own great creative ideas by refusing to visualise the project from beginning to end? When fear steps in we get muddled and indecisive and then the moment for clarity and action is (safely!) past.

Dream your dream and have the courage and confidence to confront it. Life's winners follow their instinct and their heart's desires; if a path feels 'right' for you then pursue it and see where it leads. When your life comes to an end you will want to feel that you lived well and that you loved well. Begin now to live and love your life with a great passion and flourish. The signs are there for you to follow if you are brave enough to go for what feels right for you at the deepest level of your being. Never doubt your own discretion and remember that you and only you know the right moves to make. Let your dreams show you where your heart lies and which paths you need to follow and you will live a life full of love; indeed, 'no heart has ever suffered when it goes in search of its dreams'.

EXERCISE:

How much do you love your life?

Look at the diagram over the page and give yourself a score from one to ten for each of the six indicators.

When: 1 = very poor

5 = average

10 = excellent

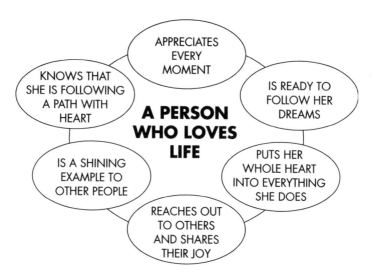

A PERSON WHO LOVES LIFE

APPRECIATES EVERY MOMENT

KNOWS THAT SHE IS FOLLOWING A PATH WITH HEART

IS READY TO FOLLOW HER DREAMS

IS A SHINING EXAMPLE TO OTHER PEOPLE

PUTS HER WHOLE HEART INTO EVERYTHING SHE DOES

REACHES OUT TO OTHERS AND SHARES THEIR JOY

If you scored 6–19

You don't need me to tell you that you are utterly low, negative and depressed. This is a very low score but please don't let this make you feel even more down. Take a positive approach and assess each indicator in turn. Where did you score very badly and why is this? For example, someone might find it impossible to reach out to others and share their joy because they have just come out of a poor relationship that has left them feeling untrusting towards others. Emotional responses like this are natural but they are only temporary.

Such a low score is an indication of deep hurt and disappointment as well as rock-bottom confidence, but all this can change! As you work on increasing your levels of confidence an amazing thing will happen; you will find that you will begin to appreciate yourself and start to trust your own judgement. As soon as this happens your world becomes a more exciting and positive place and you can begin to love your life again.

If you scored 20–29

Still a below-average score, but there are some areas where you were not totally at the bottom of the scale. Work with your most positive indicators and make them even more impressive. For example, someone who is able to communicate well with others might still find it hard to know whether they are following the right path, but by developing the skills they already have they will increase their levels of self-trust and inner-knowing. Each of the indicators in the diagram has a positive effect on all the others, so work with what you are good at and watch your self-confidence grow. Once this happens you will find it easier to develop the areas that you find more difficult. Perseverance pays; you can do this.

If you scored 30–42

You are above average and this means that you are definitely on the right track in some areas. What are your strengths? Where did you score badly? Which particular issues need attention? Focus on the fact that you are determined to be a person who loves her life; this strong intention will lead you to success. This score reflects a life where you have started to take things for granted and forgotten the bigger picture. Tap into your dreams and begin to pursue a long-term goal; this is always a great way to inject some super-positive energy into your life.

If you scored 43–60

If you are at the lower end of this score, then there is work to be done but you are aware of this. You did not achieve this high score by accident, you have been working hard on yourself and you know how to tap into your confident self. You also have a strong sense of intuition but you may not always follow it. Many congratulations to all of you in this scoring group, you are on the way and you deserve all your success. And for those of you who have a very high score, keep up the good work. You of all people know what it has taken to get you here and that you always need to keep the spark of love, enthusiasm and confidence alive; keep shining!

Forgive yourself

When you are hopeful, positive, upbeat, appreciative, forgiving and open-hearted you are demonstrating your trust and love of life. In this state you are able to feel self-respect and self-worth as you freely express your feelings, stand by your own values and walk your talk.

But this optimum state is never a permanent condition (we might wish it were). No, the reality is that life is ever changing and so are we. A human life is a work in progress, ever moving, developing and evolving, and change is our essence. When we work to increase our confidence and self-esteem, we are not striving to become the perfect human being but are striving to be our best.

Clients can be very critical and unforgiving of themselves when they are feeling less than their best, saying things like: *how could I have let myself down again, why am I so negative, how come I lost faith in myself, where did all my confidence go . . .?* But this is a dangerous path leading straight into the negative cycle of defeat. One of the most important things to know and to keep remembering is that you will go up and down; *accept this* and stop railing against it. Highs and lows are a part of life. When your fabulously confident state changes into something more challenging, don't blame yourself.

We can only ever be in the positive cycle of success or in the negative cycle of defeat; there is nothing in between. We cannot feel a bit positive or a bit negative; we are either one or the other. So the trick here is to look for self-forgiveness in your heart whenever you find yourself in a negative cycle. If you just start to beat yourself up for your pessimism and self-doubt then you will only reinforce these feelings and fulfil your negative expectations.

Forgive yourself for all your 'inadequacies'; let go of the need to be perfect or good enough – you *are* good enough. Love yourself for all your strengths and for all your frailties; these are what make you the amazing and original human that you are. When you can love all parts of yourself (the unattractive as well as the attractive) you become more tolerant and loving towards others and your confidence will automatically increase. So open your heart to love and you will open your heart to life.

INNER REFLECTION

THE WORLD HEART EMBRACE*

THIS EXERCISE HAS BEEN DESCRIBED AS THE MOST LIFE-AFFIRMING GESTURE, THE PRIMAL LOVING WELCOME OF THE ETERNAL MOTHER. MUSCLE TESTING SHOWS THAT MERELY SEEING THIS GESTURE WILL STRENGTHEN YOUR LIFE FORCE.

- Stand up and really stretch.
- Now inhale deeply and hold out your arms as wide as you can.
- Imagine that you are embracing the whole world.
- Hold the stretch and this vision as long as you can hold your breath.
- As you exhale, bring your arms slowly, gently and lovingly together so that your hands fold over each other on your chest.
- You have brought the love of the whole world into your heart; feel it enter every part of your body.
- Spend a few moments appreciating the feeling of warmth and wellbeing.
- Repeat these actions again. As you inhale and stretch, know that you are sending out love to the universe, and as you exhale and bring your hands to your chest you are receiving the love of the world.

The universal life force flows through us continually and this beautiful exercise helps us to become aware of the love inside us and around us. Start to tap into this love and you will begin to feel its amazing effects in all parts of your life. The more love you radiate the more you will attract. Look for love and you will see it everywhere.

*Adapted from my book, *Weekend Love Coach*

Step 6
Be a Winner

*She knew from an early age that she was very ill.
She was four when she told her mother that she
wanted to raise money for cancer research by
opening one of those good old American standbys,
a lemonade stand, selling lemonade in her front
garden for 50 cents a cup.*
*'Oh darling,' said her mother, 'I don't think you'll
raise much that way . . . maybe only $5 or $10.' 'I
don't care,' Alex said. 'I want to do it, anyway.'*

TAKEN FROM THE ARTICLE *A COURAGEOUS
LAST STAND*, BY BARRY WIGMORE,
THE TIMES, 8 DECEMBER 2004

A winner always makes the most of whatever she has; she
does the very best she can and maintains a positive approach
even in the face of adversity.

Alex's story
The life and times of Alex Scott (1996–2004) are a sharp
reminder of the potential courage and resilience of the
human spirit. Just before she was one, Alex was diagnosed
with neuroblastoma, an aggressive childhood cancer. Her
mother, Liz, says, 'It was her first birthday. I thought, "What
kind of life is she going to have?"'

Alex went on to have a short but remarkable life. The doctors were amazed when she quickly learned to walk after undergoing painful physiotherapy. She was clever and academically advanced despite repeated stretches of time in hospital and she had a determination and focus that drew attention. Alex opened her first lemonade stand in her front yard in 2000, with the idea of donating the proceeds to 'her hospital'. A local paper picked up the story and publicised her campaign, which raised $2,000 for the hospital where she was being treated. By 2002 local people and businesses were offering big support and one man paid a record $500 for a cup of Alex's lemonade. The willpower and courage of this little girl were such an inspiration to others and eventually led her parents to setting up a charity, the Alex's Lemonade Stand Fund. They established the website www.alexslemonade.com and the campaign went global.

In 2003 there was an Alex's Lemonade Stand Day when children throughout America (and some in France and Canada) opened lemonade stands. Volvo cars put up stands on their sales forecourts and the man who had paid $500 for his cup of lemonade the previous year paid double that price in 2003. That year Alex raised $159,000 but her dream for 2004 was to raise $1 million, and thousands of children across America rallied to the cause. As she went in and out of hospital for painful chemotherapy treatment Alex watched her lemonade fund increase from $250,000 to $700,000 and with her parents' help she wrote the book, *Alex and the Amazing Lemonade Stand* (available on www.amazon.co.uk).

In June 2004 Alex sold lemonade at a school near her home; she was weak and in a wheelchair and had to be helped by her family. Two months later she died. Her mother says: 'We had known for several days that the end was near. It was as though Alex had been determined to go to that last lemonade stand day at the school, and after that she was satisfied.'

Three months after she died Alex reached her $1 million target. Her parents are still running the Lemonade Stand Fund, which has now raised more than $1.2 million.

What a girl! What a goal! What a winner! Let Alex's story be an inspiration to you whenever you feel like giving up on your plans. You always have a chance to make a real go of whatever life has dealt you; take it! In the words of the late great playwright, Arthur Miller, 'You turn the cards over and you do the best with the hand you've got.'

10 Simple winning strategies

1   **Ask for help when you need it.** Whenever we are feeling low in confidence we are inclined to expect far too much of ourselves. Perhaps we are afraid of showing our vulnerability and neediness (in case this demonstrates a lack of self-esteem). But in reality people absolutely love to help and support others; they love to give their advice, just try them and see. Make sure that you ask in a bright, open way, for example: 'I have no idea how this works, can you help me please?' It isn't a crime to not know something and if someone acts like it is then this shows you a lot about the type of person they are. But you will find that nearly every time you reach out to others the support you need will be there. We are here to help each other, so why not give someone a chance to help you?

2   **Let go of the need to be right.** Have you ever found yourself trying to 'prove' that you are right to someone,

INSTANT BOOST

CREATE A TREASURE BOX

WHERE DO YOU PUT THOSE PRECIOUS NOTES, MEMENTOES, PHOTOS AND INSPIRING QUOTES THAT YOU HAVE PICKED UP ALONG THE WAY? MAYBE THEY ARE SCATTERED AROUND THE HOUSE OR MAYBE YOU HAVEN'T EVER BOTHERED TO COLLECT SUCH THINGS. IF YOU DON'T HAVE A PLACE TO SAVE YOUR MEMORABLE BITS AND PIECES, THEN CREATE ONE TODAY.

- LOOK OUT FOR A PRETTY BOX OR ANY SUITABLE CONTAINER. YOU COULD BUY SOMETHING SUITABLE OR EVEN DECORATE A SHOEBOX YOURSELF.
- THIS IS YOUR TREASURE BOX WHERE YOU KEEP ALL THOSE THINGS THAT ARE DEAR TO YOU AND MOVE YOUR HEART. THESE MIGHT INCLUDE: PHOTOS, YOUR CHILD'S FIRST TOOTH, A PROGRAMME FROM A SPECIAL THEATRE OUTING, A WONDERFUL POEM, AN INSPIRING QUOTATION . . .
- THIS BOX IS A MEMORY SAVER FOR YOUR FUTURE: A HEARTWARMING PLACE TO VISIT IN THE MONTHS AND YEARS AHEAD AND A GUARANTEED WAY TO REMEMBER AND RELIVE PRECIOUS MOMENTS.

perhaps a work colleague or a loved one? This can easily happen when you are having an ordinary conversation and suddenly you find yourself disagreeing. At this point we stop listening and are busy getting our argument together and looking for a chance to break into the exchange with some heated words of our own. Start to notice when you stop listening to another person because you are busy creating your reply in your head: this is an example of a time when you are needing to be right. Letting go of this need is such a liberating experience. Next time you are bursting with your own important view, just stop for a moment and recognise what you are doing. If you know you are right why would you need to convince anyone else?

The truth always emerges in the end. Stop trying to be right and you will let go of an enormous psychological and emotional burden; you will be much more fun, your relationships will improve dramatically and you will feel more confident.

3 **Understand yourself.** Why do we let our negative patterns create limitations and unhappiness in our lives? Why do we attract failure and lack of success? Of course we are not doing this consciously; in fact we are so unconscious of how we do it that we usually manage to find someone else to blame for our 'bad luck'. The truth is that we sabotage ourselves by radiating negative thoughts, emotions and behaviour patterns; in other words we think, feel and act like a loser. At the root of these patterns lies a need to destroy or belittle our achievements, because we believe that we don't deserve success. When we hold critical beliefs about ourselves we will never believe that we deserve the best and so we will never allow ourselves to have the best. If you are feeling like a loser instead of a winner you need to get to grips with your deepest self-beliefs and understand exactly how you are standing in the way of your own success. *Know thyself is* the first counsel written over

the gateway to the temple at Delphi. In knowing and understanding yourself you learn everything you need to know to create happiness and satisfaction; this is the master key to positive change.

4   **Be persistent.** Persistence is the essential quality of all winners. Anyone who has achieved a significant goal has needed truckloads of perseverance and endurance to overcome the obstacles along the way and to see things through to fruition. I mentioned the following (alleged) conversation with Thomas Edison in *Weekend Life Coach*, and because it's so good I think it deserves repeating here.

Edison was reportedly asked, 'Why do you keep trying to create an electric light bulb when you have already failed 10,000 times?' He is said to have answered that he had not failed 10,000 times; rather, that he had successfully discovered 10,000 alternatives that didn't work, and with each of these discoveries he became closer to finding the one breakthrough that would succeed. And this, of course, is exactly what he did.

We only learn by making mistakes and moving on from them. Winners meet their challenges with creativity, flexibility and determination; they look for new solutions and keep trying alternatives until they find a way that works. Each time you meet a setback and overcome it you increase your self-belief and confidence. Next time you encounter an obstacle to your plans don't crumble and fall apart but know that you can rise to the challenge; this is the way you create a win–win situation for your self. Keep going and you cannot ever lose.

5   **Be at peace with yourself.** We can run ourselves ragged with all the things we think we 'should' be doing. We

can make our lives a misery with self-blame and guilt and our identification with the 'not good enough' syndrome. Do you recognise yourself here? If so, relax; you are in the majority. However fabulous your goals and however close you are to achieving them you will always feel like a loser if you cannot accept that you are good *enough just the way you are.* It's great to enjoy your personal triumphs but they are not enough to sustain your satisfaction and happiness.

Successes alone cannot give you the fulfilment you seek. Begin to appreciate who you are at the very deepest level and you will find a quiet place inside yourself, which is always calm and centred. Winners know that it is not the goal that is most important but rather who they are becoming in the quest for their goal. Enjoy the journey!

6   **Let joy into your life.** Imagine this: you have come to a fork in the road and one route is signposted *JOY* and the other is signposted *STRUGGLE*. Which path will you take? Although it might not always feel like it, the reality is that joy and struggle are not the results of bad things happening to you; they are only attitudes, approaches and ways of seeing things, and you are always free to choose which mind-set to adopt. Why look for the negative instead of the positive? Why expect the worst rather than the best? Why be a cynic when we know that cynics never win? Why look at the mud when we can look at the stars? Why choose to be a loser and a victim when you can create a new positive reality for yourself? Think of Alex Scott and her Lemonade Stand Fund; she chose the path of joy when many others would have given up.

Choose the path of joy, just for today. Suspend your

worries and go out there and smile! When you encounter negativity just choose not to go there! Let the others complain and struggle but keep in your own calm centre. Be uplifted today and share your good feelings; the more joy you radiate the more you will attract.

7 **Learn to say 'no'.** Do you have difficulty saying this little word? We can change the complete course of our lives when we don't say 'no' when we need to. It's a word that is emotionally charged for most of us and often links with our earliest memories of rejection. But it's really only a word and a very useful one at that! Think of a time when you didn't say 'no' when you wanted to; what happened as a result? Begin to notice the times when you hold back your true feelings and say 'yes' when you want to say 'no', or say nothing and let the moment pass. Winners know what they want in life and also what they don't want and they are not afraid to voice their opinions and feelings. Next time you want to say 'no' and you find yourself saying 'yes' instead, examine your true feelings and then stop betraying them. I can promise you that saying 'no' gets easier and easier, but like most things you can only get good if you practise a lot. Be true to yourself and you will always feel like a winner.

8 **Stop apologising for yourself and your actions.** I was in the supermarket last week and I saw a man run his trolley into the back of the woman in front of him; she jumped and immediately said 'sorry' and he grumbled crossly at her and moved on. I didn't know who I was more infuriated with, the man who was so rude or the woman who invited him to be so rude.

Of course winners apologise when they hit people with trolleys but they know they don't have to say sorry every time they do anything that offends others. And they *never* say sorry for just being in the wrong place at the wrong time.

It is not your responsibility to take the blame when others don't understand you or your actions, so unless there is a positive reason to explain your motives just desist! Withhold that urge to say sorry and take the blame for everything that goes wrong and you will give others the great opportunity to treat you well rather than to victimise you.

Begin to notice the people who say sorry all the time and the effect that this has on you; irritating, isn't it? Some people feel most comfortable when they are stuck in the role of the victim and they love to take the blame (and moan about it afterwards). Winners don't get involved in such silly games; if they make a mistake they decide whether they need to apologise or not, they learn from the experience and move on.

9 **Choose the right time to discuss important issues.** This seems almost too obvious to mention but this vital subject of good timing is often overlooked. We are never at our clearest when we are fired up with emotion but this is often the time we choose to start expressing our grievances. You don't need me to tell you that this is not the best time to negotiate a favourable outcome or resolution. Winners know that there is a foolproof way to chill out and calm down before discussing important issues; they always keep their goal in mind.

Next time you are tempted to say too much at the wrong time just pause for long enough to remind yourself of your preferred outcome. If you really want a good result you will find the strength to restrain yourself until a more auspicious time. Sometimes timing really is everything!

10 **Take the lighter path** and enjoy yourself. Life's difficulties can be hard to bear and we all go through periods of darkness and loss; this is part of what being alive is all about. But sometimes even our everyday emotions become hard to handle so that we fall into that depressing cycle of defeat, and it is at this time when we need to remind ourselves that we can choose a less heavy mood. Have you noticed how seriously we take ourselves when we are feeling negative? Winners appreciate that things can be hard but they also know not to take life (and themselves) too seriously.

When we take the lighter path we are open to creative solutions and are more able to see the silver lining inside a dark cloud. It also becomes easier to get things in perspective, so that we can judge what is worth being concerned about and what is inconsequential. Expect to enjoy your day and you will find that this has a really positive effect on your confidence.

INNER REFLECTION

ONCE UPON A WINNING TIME

AFTER YOU HAVE READ THE INSTRUCTIONS BELOW, PUT THE BOOK ASIDE AND QUIETLY VISUALISE A PAST SUCCESS. CHOOSE ANYTHING WHERE YOU FELT LIKE A TRUE WINNER. AND EVEN IF YOU NEVER WON THE EGG AND SPOON RACE OR CAME TOP OF THE CLASS, THERE WILL BE AT LEAST ONE OCCASION WHERE YOU SHONE BRIGHTLY. GO BACK IN

TIME AS FAR AS YOU NEED TO. REMEMBER THAT OUR
DEFINITION OF WINNING IS NOT RESTRICTED TO BEING
FIRST BUT IT DOES INVOLVE YOU GIVING OF YOUR VERY
BEST AND REACHING YOUR POTENTIAL.

- CLOSE YOUR EYES, SLOW DOWN YOUR BREATHING AND
  LET GO OF ANY TENSION. AS YOU BEGIN TO FEEL
  CALMER AND CALMER START TO RECALL THE MEMORY OF
  YOUR GREAT SUCCESS.
- PICTURE IT IN YOUR MIND'S EYE AND BRING THE WHOLE
  OCCASION TO LIFE WITH COLOURS, DETAILS, SOUNDS
  AND FEELINGS. GET RIGHT INTO THE HEART OF THE
  SCENE AND VISUALISE YOUR TRIUMPH.
- TAP INTO ALL YOUR SENSES AND REALLY LIVE THE SCENE
  AGAIN. HOW DOES IT FEEL?
- ENLARGE THIS FEELING, MAKE IS AS POWERFUL AS YOU
  CAN AND AT THE SAME TIME 'ANCHOR' IT AT THE
  PHYSICAL LEVEL. YOU CAN DO THIS BY TOUCHING YOUR
  THUMB AND FOREFINGER TOGETHER AS YOU ALLOW
  YOURSELF TO 'FEEL' YOUR SUCCESS.
- NEXT TIME YOU FEEL YOURSELF BECOMING A VICTIM
  JUST MAKE YOUR ANCHORING SIGN AND YOU WILL
  AUTOMATICALLY TAP INTO THAT FEELING OF SUCCESS.
- REMIND YOURSELF HOW IT FEELS TO BE A WINNER AND
  BEFORE YOU KNOW IT YOU WILL BE FULL OF
  CONFIDENCE AGAIN.

Winners are attractive

'What goes around comes around.' In other words we will
attract whatever we radiate. But exactly how does this work?
And how do winners attract such good outcomes?

Modern scientific theory now endorses the ancient beliefs of mystical tradition that show that we really can *change our outer circumstances by changing our inner awareness.* Our energy is magnetic: atoms, which build life, are simply energy fields with positive, negative and neutral charges and they create electrical and magnetic forces. Electricity attracts, makes you magnetic and draws things to you. The pole that runs from north to south through the centre of the earth is magnetised, and in exactly the same way your human body is also a magnet.

Now imagine a tank full of beautiful fish; they are swimming unconsciously around in the water just as we swim unconsciously in our universal sea of electro-magnetism. Each time we have a thought it registers in the delicate and sensitive electromagnetic field that surrounds us. The laws of attraction and repulsion operate electro-magnetically; all this means is that energy of a specific type or vibration is inclined to attract energy of a similar quality and vibration, which is why we say that we attract whatever we radiate. In practice this principle demonstrates that all the things on which we focus most strongly; all the beliefs and expectations we hold and the power and strength of our imagination, all come together and draw into our lives exactly what we are giving out.

And this is why we talk of negative and positive self-fulfilling prophecies. Because our imagination follows our beliefs we constantly find ourselves in cycles of thought, feeling and behaviour that just automatically reinforce these beliefs (whether they are positive or negative). Winners generate positive self-beliefs such as *I am great; I can do it; I will give it my very best shot; I am determined and focused; I deserve the best that I can get. . . etc.* And in this way they paint mental pictures of personal success (they can *see* themselves in a positive light). These imaginings create matching emotions (feeling upbeat, motivated, enthusiastic, go-getting . . . etc.), which automatically produce an upsurge of feel-good hormones. These emotional and physical changes go on to have a direct effect on their behaviour; they become assertive and decisive and they interpret events in a favourable light and can recognise all the opportunities that are available. Winners tap into the full power of electromagnetic energy by taking the positive view every time. Look again at the Cycle of Success diagram on page 39 to see exactly how this works.

Stop and imagine that sea of universal electromagnetism that you are swimming around in, even as you are reading these words. This electromagnetic force is our life force, and the more we can absorb the more 'alive' we will become. We have an incredible 72,000 nerve centres destined for the trans-mission of electromagnetic energy and it is said that we use roughly only 5,000 of them. Which poses this great question for us all: How much more fabulously alive can we get then?

Deep breathing, joyfulness, positive thinking, appreciation, relaxation and meditation practices all help us to open up more of these energetic points. But the most powerful way for us to access this life force is so simple and direct. All we need do is become aware of this potent energy and immerse ourselves in it: living it, loving it, radiating it and of course, attracting it.

EXERCISE:

How attractive are you?

No, this has nothing to do with the size of your bum or the number of your wrinkles or the dryness of your hair or any other body image issues you might have. This question is really asking: 'How much electromagnetic energy do you attract?' Are you buzzing with life and crackling with static or are your batteries flat?

Perhaps you have heard of the concept of 'stickiness'. This is a term that is used on the Internet to describe the success rate of a website to attract repeat visitors. If a website is described as 'sticky' it means that it attracts people again and again. Think about your ability to attract the life force (positive energy) into your experiences.

- Remember a time when you were feeling powerful and in charge. How did you act? How did you speak? What was your outcome? In other words, what did you attract to yourself and exactly how did you attract it?
- Now think of a time when your energy was low and your negative expectations were fulfilled. Can you remember how you acted and how you spoke? What sort of outcome did you attract and why did you attract it?
- Next time you are feeling low in personal energy just remember that you can turn this situation around immediately. Uplift yourself and your future prospects by tapping into a positive view of yourself and your expectations. In this way you can step into the cycle of success, which is only a positive thought away.

When you close off and forget your own amazing potential those positive feelings, upbeat people and great chances and lucky breaks will all drop away from you (you will lose your stickiness) and you will feel their lack as you sink into negativity. On the other hand, if you keep open and aware then positivity in all its forms will stick to you repeatedly.

INNER REFLECTION

ABSORBING THE LIFE FORCE*

SIT QUIETLY AND THINK ABOUT YOUR 72,000 NERVE CENTRES. IF WE CAN USE THEM ALL WE WOULD INCREASE OUR ENERGY INTAKE BY MORE THAN FOURTEEN TIMES.

REMEMBER HOW YOU FEEL STANDING AT THE SEASHORE AND TAKING IN GREAT LUNGFULS OF AIR; IT'S SO UPLIFTING AND REVITALISING, ISN'T IT? NO MATTER WHERE YOU ARE, YOU CAN LIFT YOUR ENERGY AND ABSORB MORE OF THE LIFE FORCE BY SIMPLY BECOMING CONSCIOUS OF YOUR BREATHING.

- AS YOU TAKE DEEPER AND FULLER BREATHS, FEEL THE CHANGES IN YOUR ENERGY. NOTICE HOW IT FEELS TO BE MORE OPEN AND AWARE.
- SPEND THE REST OF TODAY REMEMBERING YOUR CAPACITY TO INCREASE YOUR ENERGY.
- VISUALISE THOSE 72,000 NERVE CENTRES SHIMMERING THROUGHOUT YOUR BODY; THEY ARE THERE FOR YOU TO USE, SO BECOME AWARE OF THEM.

AS YOU ABSORB MORE OF THE ENERGY OF THE UNIVERSE YOU WILL RADIATE POSITIVITY IN EVERYTHING YOU DO AND SO YOU WILL BECOME A NATURAL MAGNET FOR ALL THE GOOD THINGS OF LIFE.

*ADAPTED FROM MY BOOK, *JUST DO IT NOW!*

Step 7
Take Positive Action

Lynda, I just don't know where to start. I'm feeling so low in confidence that I can't trust myself to know how to act and every decision feels so hard, to make. How can I get focused and motivated and go for my goals when I don't know what I really want? How can I start to take charge of my life when I'm so muddled and uncertain about everything? Really, I think my only goal is to get confident so that I can feel good about myself and then maybe everything will fall into place.

A CLIENT

This quote is taken from an email from a life coaching client, and I get emails just like this every day. So if you are feeling muddled, confused and dazed by life in general then take a step back and just relax; you are not alone!

When confidence plummets and you get drawn into a negative cycle where everything seems impossible *there are many ways out*! Perhaps this is the most important and vital thing to remember when the going is tough and everything feels like it's falling apart. Recognise that a negative condition is only a temporary state of mind and that it will pass.

Of course you can hasten its passing by using any of the tips and techniques that we have been looking at in the book so far, and as soon as you do this you will get moving into the positive cycle.

Being positive is not about always saying you are 'fine' when you are not; continually smiling when you are in emotional pain; letting others get away with bad behaviour and generally not being true to your feelings. A positive person is a realist: she knows that things are always changing and that dark clouds will pass, but she also knows that sometimes life is hard and can be hurtful. Being positive is about combining an optimistic and openhearted approach together with a realistic take on what is going on.

No one has an easy life, although sometimes this might seem to be the case. On a low day when we are inclined to compare ourselves unflatteringly with every person we meet, it is easy to imagine that we are the only ones with troubles. Everyone has to face their own problems and insecurities; we all suffer losses and grief and emotional pain so we might as well accept this and learn how to deal with these feelings. When we can be positive in the face of seemingly negative situations we develop great inner strength and internal resources that give us confidence for the future. And this is really what we mean when we talk about feeling in charge of our lives: we know that we can face the good times and the bad *and still survive*.

On a day when you just don't know where to turn there is only one solution: turn to yourself. You are the only one who can solve your problems; no one else can do this for you. Others might listen to you, give good advice and be supportive, but they can never resolve your own issues. It is tempting to look outside ourselves for the strength we need but actually we can only ever find that strength within.

10 Ways to take positive action when the going gets rough

1 **Remember that nothing is impossible.** You can and will see this through, one way or another, with the skill and grace that you have used many times before.

2 **Recognise that you are in the negative cycle** and that is why you are feeling unsure and insecure. You have only to move into a positive cycle and things will look lighter and brighter immediately.

3 **Take a tip from this book!** You could make a positive affirmation, take a risk, make some time for yourself, activate a plan, declutter your wardrobe, tell someone how much you love them, go for a walk in the countryside... do anything that will move your energy in a positive way.

4 **Be realistic.** This means looking coolly at your predicament and assessing exactly what needs to be done.

5 **Make a decision.** And if you are feeling too muddled to do this just look at *any possible decision* and see how it feels. Pretend that you are going to take a course of action and then imagine how you would react after you had taken it. If it feels wrong then you know it would be the wrong move. Keep trying different possibilities until one of them 'feels right' deep down in your gut; *this is the one to take!*

6 **Get things down on paper.** This is a very good way to clear your mind and see how you can move forward. What steps do you need to take? Which is the first step? How can you take it? When will you take it?

7 **Commit yourself to making the necessary changes.** Make a contract with yourself, *I will take this step by ... I*

will take the next step by. . . give yourself real deadlines and stick to them.

8 **Know that the universe supports you.** Whenever you strive to improve your situation, unseen forces come to your aid. When you tap into your own positive energy you are linking with the universal life force and attracting all the positivity that you will need.

9 **Take that first step towards an important goal.** Choose a meaningful long-term goal and begin. Do it now. Put down this book and do whatever it takes to start to get this show on the road. Now how do you feel?

10 **Treat yourself compassionately.** Think of yourself as a wonderful person who is struggling to do her best even when she is low in confidence and feeling fearful. Admire her strength of will and determination; isn't she brave and persevering? Yes, you are a true inspiration to yourself.

Melinda's story

Melinda, 34, is a single mother to Charlie, aged 6. She met me when I was running a confidence-building workshop and afterwards decided to have some personal coaching.

Melinda told me that although she loved Charlie her life as a single mum was eroding her self-confidence and self-belief. She said that she 'muddled through' her days and every night went to bed feeling exhausted, inadequate and resentful. Parenting is such a hugely responsible and challenging job and going it alone can be so stressful and pressurising. I felt that someone needed to acknowledge the good job that Melinda was doing and asked her about her social circle. She said that she felt quite alone and that all Charlie's friends at school lived with both their parents and she felt awkward

INSTANT BOOST

KNOW YOUR OUTCOME

You will never be able to reach a goal unless you have already specified it. It's a bit like going on a journey with no particular destination: how would you ever know when you had arrived?

When you know your outcome:

- It helps to keep you on track.
- You are focused on a goal.
- The steps you need to take become obvious to you.
- It becomes easier to make a plan and to stick to it.
- You will feel motivated each time you visualise your objective.
- You can measure your progress. (how near am I to achieving my outcome?)
- As you get nearer and nearer to achieving your specified goal you will feel more and more confident.
- Your increasing levels of confidence will lead you to new horizons.
- Others will recognise your focus and commitment and will become increasingly supportive.
- You can measure your success and celebrate your achievement.
- One fulfilled outcome just leads to another and another and . . .

about pursuing friendships with them.

I asked Melinda to work with the **10 Ways to take positive action,** on page 112. She struggled immediately with number **1, Remember that nothing is impossible.** She asked me how she could possibly make a go of her life when she had made so many 'mistakes' and felt like she could never be a 'good enough' mum to Charlie? We looked back at the last seven years and how she had dealt with being pregnant and being alone and then how she had brought up Charlie to be the lovely child that he was. And yes, she could see that she had shown great resourcefulness and creativity in facing her challenges. Being a parent requires stamina, humour, self-belief and a positive frame of mind and Melinda agreed that she had shown all these qualities.

Using the **10 Ways to take positive action** Melinda was able to create some simple action plans which led to great changes in her life. She decided to join the local branch of Gingerbread, which is an association that offers support to single parents. This opened her door to a great new social life and she became more and more confident. By the end of two months Melinda had created a step-by-step action plan, which led to her taking a part-time job at Charlie's school. At the end of our sessions Melinda had this to say: 'I didn't realise how hard I was being on myself, it was almost like I felt I didn't deserve to be happy. Taking these positive steps has shown me that it is possible to start to believe in myself and this has led to new friendships and a new job. I think it's fair to say that the most important thing is to be more compassionate with yourself. I have stopped telling myself off and blaming myself for everything; this only made me feel terrible and made me ineffective. I hope my story will help anyone else who is reading this to be kinder to themselves and to take some positive action because it will change your life for the better.'

Confidence quiz

Choose answers A or B and see how confident you are.

1 You wake up and it's a bad hair day!
  A Your day is ruined; you can never feel your best if you don't look good.
  B You do the best you can to look OK and then you forget all about it.

2 You are going on a job interview.
  A You are nervous and think that you don't stand a chance.
  B You are nervous but you know that's quite natural. You feel optimistic because you got through to the interview level and you know you can do the job.

3 You make plans for an outing with a friend and at the very last minute she phones to cancel.
  A You say, 'that's fine' but you are all dressed up with nowhere to go and you feel cross.
  B You ask her why she couldn't let you know earlier and you don't automatically agree to go out with her next time she asks.

4 It's Friday night and your boss has asked you to stay late (again!).

A You say 'of course' and put your head down but inside you are fuming.

B You say, 'I can do it this time but in future I will need more notice.'

5 A friend introduces you to a new man and encourages you to go on a date with him but you don't fancy him.

A You feel intimidated when he rings and you agree to meet him.

B When he rings to ask you out you say that you would rather not.

6 A colleague keeps asking you questions about your private life, which you find intrusive.

A You don't want to hurt her feelings so you tell her details which you would rather keep to yourself.

B You tell her that this information is confidential and you feel uncomfortable talking about it.

7 A new girl has joined your social circle and she is always moaning and complaining about other people.

A You just put up with it because the others don't seem to mind.

B You mention how you feel to your friends and go out only on nights when she doesn't come.

8 Life is in overdrive and you feel like a hamster in a wheel.

A You just keep going, rushing here and there until you collapse in a heap.

B You calm down and look for ways that others might be able to help you; then you ask for their help.

9 Someone is criticising you, telling you what you 'should' and 'shouldn't' be doing.

    A You just sit and take it.

    B You tell the person that you have no wish to listen to his criticisms and if he doesn't stop you remove yourself.

10 You are faced with a difficult decision and you don't know which path to take.

    A Someone you admire gives you their advice, and although you are still not sure you take it.

    B You listen to the advice of others and weigh up the pros and cons until you come to a decision that *you* are happy with.

11 You are struggling with your self-image and wish you could be thinner, taller, blonder . . . or whatever.

    A This issue continually preys on your mind and you keep wishing you looked like someone else.

    B You do the best you can to look and feel great and then just get on and have a good time.

12 There is something you would really like to achieve and you know that it will change your life, but it will take some time and also some commitment.

    A You will wait until you feel more ready to go for your goal.

    B You want this and you are ready to take the leap; you cannot keep your life on hold.

13 You make a mistake which has had bad consequences for you.

    A You can't stop thinking about it and keep wishing that

you had behaved differently; you are cross with yourself.

B Yes, you made a silly error but you won't let it hold you back. You know that you will learn from this and never make the same mistake again.

14 Someone is gossiping about you behind your back and you are feeling uncomfortable.

A You get very upset and keep wondering what others think about you.

B You know that you have done nothing wrong and if others think badly of you then they are no friends of yours.

15 Family members have thrown their belongings around the house.

A You pick them up.

B You tell them to pick them up.

Score 1 for each time you answered A. Score 2 for each time you answered B.

If you scored 15–19

Your confidence is low but you don't need me to tell you that. There are many times in a day when you automatically put the needs of others before your own. Ask yourself why you do this.

When you feel too afraid to stand up for yourself you often end up feeling resentful and angry with yourself and with others. You are probably afraid of what people think and you often find it very hard to say 'no' and to make any clear decisions. What a high price you are paying for refusing to take that confident step into the centre of your life; is it worth it?

What to do

Think of a situation that you really want to confront. What is it that you want to say and to whom? Imagine meeting this person and saying your piece and then get out there and do it for real. I know this will make you feel so good about yourself. Remember that your feelings are just as important as the next person's.

If you scored 20–24

There are times when you act with confidence but then you get overwhelmed with self-doubt and you lose it again. You are supersensitive to criticism from others and this hurts you and brings you down a lot of the time. When things go wrong you are inclined to take the blame and this makes you doubt yourself. You have some long-term goals that you often think about but you feel frightened at the thought of actually going for them. You know yourself quite well and would love to be the person you know you can be.

What to do

Stop sitting around thinking and analysing and contemplating your navel; just *do something* that you long to do. You will never be confident if you are afraid to take a risk; overcoming challenges makes us strong and self-assured. Go ahead and feel the fear and then do it anyway; the next step will be easy. You are the only thing standing in your way.

If you scored 25–30

Congratulations, you stand out from the crowd. You understand the power of self-belief and you know that you deserve to be treated well. You are discriminating and will not spend time with negative and critical people and you attract respect from others. Confidence develops from a positive can-do attitude and you know this and are always prepared to go that extra mile. When you feel low it is not the end of your world; you know that bad things sometimes happen to good people and that there are times when we have to ride the storm.

What to do
Just keep doing what you are doing! You above all people know how hard you have worked to reach this level of self-esteem and confidence and you also know that you have to keep doing this work in order to stay upbeat.

Get specific

Sometimes clients tell me that they feel more confident in one area of their lives than others. For example, they might find it easy to be assertive in the workplace but have very little confidence in a social setting. Or maybe they have a great intimate relationship but still struggle with their self-image and body confidence.

Although it's true to say that we *can* be more assertive in one area of our life than another, long experience shows me that *real* self-confidence spills out into every single one of our experiences. In other words, a sense of calm self-assurance will have a hugely positive effect in all our life zones: our work, intimate and family relationships, our self-image and body confidence and any other area.

The most useful way to weed out the inhibitions, doubts and worries that stop us feeling superconfident is to get specific about our satisfaction levels in every area of our life. Check out your present satisfaction levels in the Life Zone Checklist below.

The scale of feelings from 1 to 8 represents the range of emotions from your lowest to your highest satisfaction levels. No need to think long and hard about your answers, just tick off the number that most relates to your feelings.

High satisfaction levels

8 Thrilled, fulfilled, delighted
7 Very satisfied
6 Pleased, positive
5 Moderately satisfied
4 Sometimes OK and sometimes not
3 Dissatisfied, unfulfilled
2 Unhappy, negative
1 Totally flat, depressed, miserable

Low satisfaction levels

SCALE OF FEELINGS

LIFE ZONE	1	2	3	4	5	6	7	8
LOVE								
FAMILY								
CAREER								
MONEY								
FRIENDS								
SELF-IMAGE								
HEALTH AND FITNESS								
HOBBIES AND PERSONAL INTERESTS								

LIFE ZONE CHECKLIST

Any answers below 6 need investigating. Why would you be putting up with anything that is less than pleasing and positive? Of course some of your scores will be less than 6, which is quite normal. But you have greater expectations for yourself, don't you? Why ever else would you be reading this book?

Don't let any poor results affect your self-esteem. Use this important information to show you the specific areas that you need to work on in order to gain total confidence. Write your results and any consequent thoughts and feelings in your journal and we will come back to this later.

INSTANT BOOST

STEP INTO YOUR CONFIDENT SHOES

CONSIDER YOUR FEELINGS AT THE MOMENT. THINK ABOUT HOW YOUR CONFIDENCE LEVELS AFFECT EACH AREA OF YOUR LIFE.

- HOW DOES LOW SELF-CONFIDENCE HOLD YOU BACK?
- WOULD YOUR LIFE BE DIFFERENT IF YOU BELIEVED IN YOURSELF?
- EXACTLY HOW WOULD IT BE DIFFERENT?
- HOW DO YOU LOOK WHEN YOU ARE LOW IN CONFIDENCE? DOES IT AFFECT YOUR BODY IMAGE; YOUR VOICE; YOUR POSTURE, YOUR ABILITY TO SMILE?
- WHEN YOU ARE FEELING GOOD ABOUT YOURSELF, NOTHING STANDS IN YOUR WAY; WHAT DOES THIS FEEL LIKE?
- HOW DO YOU WALK WHEN YOU FEEL LIKE THIS? DOES

YOUR BODY LANGUAGE CHANGE? HOW DOES YOUR
VOICE SOUND WHEN YOU ARE BUZZING WITH
CONFIDENCE? DO YOU SMILE MORE OFTEN?

- NOW BEGIN TO ADOPT THE POSE AND POISE OF A
  CONFIDENT PERSON (HOWEVER LOW YOU FEEL).

- ACT CONFIDENTLY; WALK CONFIDENTLY, SPEAK
  CONFIDENTLY, THINK CONFIDENTLY.

- STEP INTO YOUR CONFIDENT SHOES AND NOTICE THE
  EFFECT THIS HAS ON EVERYONE YOU MEET.

- ON A LOW DAY JUST 'PRETEND' TO BELIEVE IN
  YOURSELF BY STEPPING INTO YOUR CONFIDENT SHOES.
  BEFORE YOU KNOW IT YOU WILL BE FEELING SO MUCH
  BETTER ABOUT YOURSELF.

SOME CLIENTS LIKE TO IMAGINE THEIR CONFIDENT SHOES
IN GREAT DETAIL SO THAT THEY CAN EASILY VISUALISE
THEMSELVES WEARING THEM. MINE ARE RED AND SHINY
WITH *VERY* HIGH HEELS, WHAT DO YOURS LOOK LIKE?

One good plan can change your life

Confident people know where they are going and (within
limits) how they are going to get there. When clients start
outlining their plans to me I know they are feeling more
positive and open-minded: in effect they are confirming that
they believe in their goals and that they *can* and *will* go for
their outcome.

Helen's story

Helen, 27, was a personnel officer, sharing a house with
friends and feeling like a change when she met Tim. He was
tall, dark and handsome, five years older than Helen and he

worked in finance. After they had been seeing each other for about a year Tim started suggesting that they move in together. Helen felt very undecided but instead of exploring these feelings she eventually agreed to rent a flat with Tim. From the start it was a fiasco. Students rented the flat above and most nights they partied until the small hours. It also soon became obvious that Tim was no domestic god or even a new man: he ignored all housework duties and seemed quite happy to live in a pigsty. After three months of cleaning up after Tim, Helen contacted me.

She said that she just didn't know what to do and when I asked her what she wanted she was floored. 'I don't know any more, I mean I do love Tim but he is such a slob. I hate the flat as we never have any peace and I'm fed-up being his slave but mainly I am bored at work and I think this makes me more intolerant when I get home.'

I asked Helen to explain her initial reservations about moving in with Tim and she said: 'When I met him I was feeling dissatisfied and looking for a change; he just appeared at the right time. But looking back now I think that I should have stayed in my own place and put my efforts into a career move. I never had a clear plan of what I wanted and so I just sort of drifted into the next thing (which happened to be Tim). Looking after the flat and living with Tim takes up so much of my time that I can't seem to think clearly about my future.'

Well, when we got back to basics and a discussion of where her priorities lay, Helen began to get clearer. Some clients come for life coaching with a ready-formed goal (e.g. 'I want to lose weight'), but most people are quite unclear about what they want. And this is why they want coaching: to clarify where they are coming from, where they want to go, and exactly what they need to do to get there. Helen saw that her 'drifting' into situations was a sign of her indecision and lack of focus. I asked her to name the one thing she wanted most and she immediately replied, 'a new job'. When we pursued this idea she revealed that she was very keen on floral design and had always imagined that she would one day set up her own floristry business.

Helen's goal for the week was to investigate any floristry courses that would be suitable for her. By the end of the week she had found somewhere in Surrey that offered beginners, and advanced classes and she had already signed up for a Foundation Course in Flower Design. And this one plan knocked the whole of her life into shape. In one month she had left Tim and moved back with her friends and was planning to take a Diploma in Floristry Management. As soon as Helen focused on a dream goal she found the energy, clarity and motivation to get her whole life in order. She said that she suddenly seemed to lose interest in Tim and couldn't imagine why she had been putting up with him for so long. Helen made a very interesting observation when she said, 'I think I prioritised being in a relationship (almost any relationship) so that I wouldn't have to face the fact that I wasn't moving forward in my life. I don't think I ever loved Tim, I just loved the excuse he provided so that I didn't have to take the career move.'

One good plan can put you back in charge of your life, and no good plan will leave you undecided, unsure and lacking in confidence. Are you working towards a goal? Do you have a plan or are you drifting about in a cloud of uncertainty? What about those dream goals? Do they feel far away or could you start to take a step towards one of them today?

INNER REFLECTION

YOU ARE IN CONTROL

GET INTO A RELAXED AND CALM STATE AND GENTLY REVIEW YOUR LIFE.

- CONSIDER YOUR ANSWERS TO THE LIFE ZONE CHECKLIST ON PAGE 122; WHERE DID YOU SCORE LESS THAN 6?
- TAKE AN OBJECTIVE VIEW OF YOUR ANSWERS AND ASK YOURSELF, 'WHAT CAN I DO TO IMPROVE THIS AREA OF MY LIFE?'
- REMAIN WITH THIS DETACHED VIEW AND CONSIDER EXACTLY WHAT ACTIONS YOU WOULD NEED TO TAKE.
- NOW STEP INTO YOUR CONFIDENT SHOES (PAGE 123); SEE YOURSELF IN THEM AND DO A LITTLE DANCE.
- IMAGINE YOURSELF IN YOUR MAGIC SHOES, TAKING THE ACTION YOU NEED TO TAKE. VISUALISE YOURSELF STEPPING FORWARD WITH POSITIVE, UPBEAT STEPS; YOU KNOW THAT YOU CANNOT FAIL.
- FEEL THE CONFIDENT ENERGY RUNNING THROUGHOUT YOUR BODY – YES, YOU REALLY CAN GO FOR YOUR GOALS.
- HOW DOES IT FEEL TO BE FULL OF CONFIDENCE? HOLD THIS FEELING; REMEMBER IT IN DETAIL SO THAT YOU CAN RETURN TO IT WHENEVER YOU NEED TO.
- CONFIDENCE IS A STATE OF MIND – STEP INTO IT AND FEEL THE DIFFERENCE!

Part Two

CONFIDENCE FOR LIFE

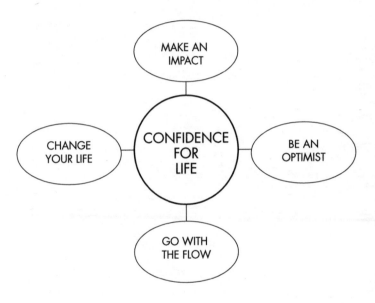

Make an Impact

Every time I wore that dress – which was practically every time I went out – I felt sensational, sexy, svelte, ritzy, elegant, early Lauren Bacall. The cut was terrific. People remarked on my figure. I'd throw on the dress, slip on my highest heeled Sergio Rossi shoes, grab my black crocodile Cartier clutch bag, and sail out of the front door just beaming with confidence. When you're from Leigh-on-Sea and the summit of your sartorial ambition for years was to 'blend in', I can't tell you the kind of buzz I get from that 'Yes, I've Got It' feeling.

MARCELLE D'ARGY SMITH,
WRITING IN THE *DAILY MAIL*

Yes indeed, we all get a buzz from that 'I've got it' feeling. The important question is, what does it for you? How can *you* get to feel that good?

When you feel good you look good and when you look good you feel good. Remember the last time you fell in love? *That's* the intensity of feeling we are talking about here; when you are glowing inside and out, you are walking on air and oozing self-confidence. But you don't have to be in love with a man to feel this good about yourself and your life; you can feel absolutely fabulous by just tuning into the real you.

A woman who knows herself carries a sense of inner security and self-awareness that shines out from her whether she is wearing a dress by Zandra Rhodes or a pair of tracksuit pants from Asda. Have you noticed how some people just stand out from the crowd whatever they are wearing? And very often these people are not even conventionally good looking, but somehow they catch the eye and make an impact wherever they go. The good news is that if they can tap into this charismatic energy then so can you.

The word charisma comes from Charis, one of the Three Graces in Greek mythology, and it used to have a theological meaning: the divine gifts or attributes we each have within us. The reality is this: as soon as you stop trying to be someone else and begin to tune into your own uniqueness and originality you start to generate your personal charisma, and wherever you go you make a stunning impact. Confidence is the most alluring quality and you cannot buy it, but you can certainly create it. The most attractive woman in the room is the one who can just be herself: she knows her own strengths and weaknesses; she has self-respect and so generates respect from others and, most importantly, she is at home in her own skin: you can be this woman!

Your personal magnetism

We have already seen how we can increase the electro-magnetic energy that we attract and radiate. Look again at the exercise called *How attractive are you?* on page 107. As you increase your own personal life force you become a natural magnet to others. Everyone is drawn to the person who is

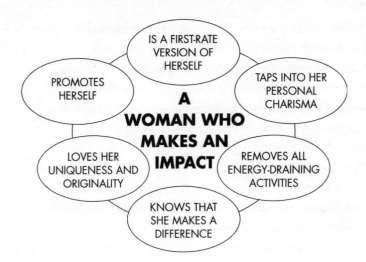

A WOMAN WHO MAKES AN IMPACT

openly enjoying and valuing her life and who is happy to demonstrate her appreciation of others.

Think of your magnetic field as a reflection of your aliveness and energy levels. Just how energised and buzzing are you right now? Give yourself a quick score out of ten, if ten is 'I feel fabulous' and one is 'I am totally flat'. Most of you will be scoring well below ten; so don't get disheartened. Instead take a look at the following list of possible energy drainers to discover exactly what might be depleting your own magnetic field.

Energy-draining activities

Negative thinking

You know that this is always bad news. As soon as you indulge in this you lose your calm self-assuredness and begin to sound like a loser – not a good image! When you catch yourself wallowing around in the negative cycle of defeat just ask yourself, 'Do I really want to be in this state? Am I sounding and looking good?' This should be enough to zap you out of your pessimistic mind-set. Your thoughts are only as real as the energy you give to them.

Blaming others

This really puts people off you as well as cutting you off from your own creative powers. Confident people are high in 'can-do' energy because they take total responsibility for their personal circumstances. Look at it this way: if someone else is to blame for the position you find yourself in then you are left helplessly waiting for them to act on your behalf. Blaming energy is unattractive and creates all-lose situations.

Trying to be like someone else

This is such a tiring and futile exercise. Every time you wish you looked like . . . or want to be like . . ., you are denying your own specialness. It's OK to have role models but it's not OK to be continually dissatisfied with what you are and what you have to offer. Decide to become a first-rate version of yourself and life will get so much simpler and more interesting. When you have the confidence to be yourself you no longer feel the need to compete with others to prove that you are worthy. Believe me, you are worth it, *just the way you are.*

Having regrets

So you made a mistake and you wish you hadn't! But if there is nothing you can do about it now at least accept this one benefit: *learn from it.* One of the most obvious features of a confident person is their ability to learn from personal faults and then to let go of them. If you are living in the past you are in the wrong time zone; shake off those cobwebs and get into the present moment, which is where the real powerful action is.

Feeling resentment

This ties up so much of your energy in a useless and totally negative activity. If you are feeling resentful of anyone at the moment just stop and look at it logically. What good are you doing? What harm are you doing to yourself? Every time you have an angry thought about another person you increase your bitterness quotient, and that is all that you do. You don't need me to tell you that anger and sourness will always make the wrong impact.

Being critical

Whether you are self-critical or are judging others you will diminish yourself. Have you noticed how the most unpopular people are the most critical? You cannot and will not show yourself off to advantage if you are looking for the worst in yourself or in others. If you know that you are inclined to do this, stop immediately. When you are tempted to say something negative about another person just *don't*. As my dad says, 'If you can't find anything nice to say about someone then don't say anything.'

Stop all energy-draining activities and you will find that your energy levels will shoot up; you will also feel lighter and brighter and more optimistic. As your electromagnetic energy increases you will notice that you are attracting new and interesting people and opportunities, and you will find it easier to resolve personal difficulties.

Take a moment here to 'tune into' your personal energy

field. Imagine that your aura is shining bright and crackling with electricity. *Feel* the energy surrounding your physical body and become aware of it as you move about your daily business. You take your vibrations with you wherever you go so make sure they are good vibrations!

Know what you've got to offer

Years ago in Cornwall when I worked as a career coach, I used to run a workshop activity called '*Make an impact*'. Cornwall is a place with high unemployment levels and any good job attracts a huge number of applicants.

The questions for any prospective job applicant are always: *How do I stand out from the crowd? What will make my CV different from everyone else's? How can I make an impact?* Employers are usually looking for positive people with great communication skills and the ability to work independently as well as with a team. But how is it possible to show that you have the relevant skills when you are constrained by the limits of your CV or by a fifteen-minute interview?

Although the workshop itself was called, '*How to get that job*', it actually always revolved around issues of self-confidence. I watched perfectly good applicants fail to get an interview because they couldn't sell themselves on paper. And then there were countless others who fell at the interview stage because they just couldn't make the right impression. My job was to motivate these people and to encourage and support their jobsearch activities by increasing their levels of self-belief.

When we feel good about ourselves it shows and it inspires confidence in others. And whether you are looking

INSTANT BOOST

STEP INTO THE WINNING CIRCLE

STAND UP AND IN YOUR MIND'S EYE DRAW A CIRCLE OF WHITE LIGHT ON THE FLOOR IN FRONT OF YOU. THIS IS YOUR WINNING CIRCLE AND AS SOON AS YOU STEP INTO IT YOU WILL BE FILLED WITH POSITIVE MAGNETIC ENERGY.

- 'SEE' THE CIRCLE OF WHITE LIGHT.
- PREPARE YOURSELF BY SAYING THE FOLLOWING MANTRA:
  I AM A WINNER
- WHEN YOU ARE READY, STEP INTO THE CIRCLE OF LIGHT.
- VISUALISE YOURSELF FILLING WITH SPARKLING WHITE LIGHT. YOUR ENERGY FEELS STRONG, POWERFUL AND ELECTRIC.
- IMAGINE THAT YOU ARE RADIATING THIS INCREDIBLE ENERGY AND THAT YOU ARE ATTRACTING POSITIVITY INTO EVERY AREA OF YOUR LIFE.
- DISSOLVE THE CIRCLE.
- KNOW THAT YOU ARE SPECIAL AND AMAZING AND THAT YOU NOW TAKE THIS ENERGY WITH YOU WHEREVER YOU GO.

YOU CAN STEP INTO YOUR WINNING CIRCLE WHENEVER YOU NEED A LIFT; IT ONLY TAKES A MOMENT.

for a job, a new relationship or you just want to feel great, positive self-belief will always give you a charismatic buzz (and who can resist this?).

There were two exercises that we did in this workshop that were of great value to the participants and I know that they will be of use to you, so why not give them a try?

EXERCISE A:

Write your own personal ad

Think of yourself as a product that you are trying to sell. Now what are your unique selling points? What have you got to offer? How can you best promote yourself?

If your self-advertisement was going into the *Daily Mail* tomorrow (circulation 2.5 million) what would it say? You have 250 words to sell your charms, strengths and talents. Use only positive statements and don't be shy, no one else needs to see this. If you are feeling stuck just think back to past successes and consider the personal qualities that you demonstrated. Remember that 'success' doesn't just refer to work or to material gain. Perhaps you are a good friend and confidante who can put people at their ease; this is a great social skill and is the type of positive quality that should definitely be included in your ad. Think long and hard about yourself and jot down any ideas and thoughts that you might have. Now write your advertisement in your journal.

Be your own PR girl

Next, find a full-length mirror and read out your advertisement.
Imagine that you are live on national TV and that 5 million
people are watching you. Read your piece. Feeling silly and
embarrassed? Read it again. Repeat this until you are feeling
relaxed and are projecting yourself with confidence. Notice how
your body language changes as you feel more self-assured.

In my career coaching workshops the participants had to do
this exercise in front of each other and it always caused plenty of
emotion to flow. Some people would refuse to do it, and then
(after hearing the brave ones) they would find the energy and
confidence to read out their piece.

If you want to make an impact then self-promotion is absolutely
vital. Start to get into the habit of talking yourself up instead of
down. This means the end to all self-deprecation. Confident
people *never* bring themselves down when in conversation with
others. And don't think that you will sound like a show-off if you
project only a positive self-image. If you sound confident, you
look confident and others will admire and respect this. On a day
when you are not feeling so brilliant just take out your ad and
read it out aloud, you will be surprised by how uplifted you will
feel. Yes, you are amazing, even on a low day; you only need to
remind yourself of this.

INNER REFLECTION

REMEMBERING THAT YOU *DO* MAKE A DIFFERENCE

ALTHOUGH THE WORLD IS A BIG PLACE AND IT'S EASY TO FEEL SMALL AND INSIGNIFICANT IN THE GRAND SCHEME OF THINGS, YOU NEED TO REMEMBER THAT EVERY SINGLE CONTRIBUTION YOU MAKE DOES COUNT.

THE STARFISH STORY REMINDS US THAT EVERY POSITIVE ACTION IS MEANINGFUL AND THAT EACH OF US CAN MAKE A DIFFERENCE.

ONE DAY A MAN WAS WALKING ALONG THE BEACH AND HE SAW THOUSANDS AND THOUSANDS OF STARFISH WASHED UP ON THE SHORE. IN THE DISTANCE HE COULD SEE A LITTLE GIRL PICKING UP A STARFISH AND THROWING IT BACK INTO THE SEA. HE WATCHED HER DO THIS OVER AND OVER AGAIN AND WHEN HE CAME NEAR TO HER HE SAID, 'YOU ARE WASTING YOUR TIME, THERE ARE TOO MANY TO THROW BACK. WHAT DIFFERENCE DO YOU THINK YOU ARE MAKING, THEY ARE ALL GOING TO DIE.' AND THE LITTLE GIRL JUST PICKED UP ANOTHER STARFISH AND AS SHE TOSSED IT INTO THE SEA SHE SAID, 'IT MAKES A DIFFERENCE *TO* THAT ONE.'

THINK ABOUT THE SIGNIFICANT PEOPLE IN YOUR LIFE: YOUR FRIENDS, FAMILY, WORK COLLEAGUES, LOVED ONES . . . REFLECT UPON EACH OF YOUR RELATIONSHIPS AND CONSIDER WHAT DIFFERENCE YOU MAKE TO THAT

PERSON'S LIFE. WHAT DO YOU GIVE THAT IS OF VALUE? WHO DO YOU HELP AND ENCOURAGE? WHAT PRACTICAL ASSISTANCE DO YOU GIVE OTHERS? DO YOU OFFER EMOTIONAL SUPPORT? ARE YOU A GOOD FRIEND? ARE YOU A GOOD LISTENER? WHO LOVES YOU AND WOULD MISS YOU?

You've got it!

You have got whatever it takes to make an impact. No need to try to blend in or to copy someone else or to lose yourself in the crowd; just begin to connect with the real and individual you and your life will begin to take off. There is no one else like you on the planet: you are totally unique; a one-off; an original design. How does this feel? Are you enthused and excited by your exclusivity or are you feeling a little lost and wondering what this might mean for you? Try the following checklist and see how happy you are to embrace your uniqueness.

EXERCISE:

Uniqueness checklist

Answer yes or no to the following questions.

1 Do you think that it is important to fit in?
2 Are you attracted to originality and creativity?
3 Do you ever use the words 'normal' or 'average' to describe yourself?
4 Are you excited by change?
5 Do you ever deny your feelings or opinions to please others?

6 Do the achievements and talents of others daunt you?

7 Is it important for you to keep up with fashion trends?

8 Do you ever feel different from others in some way?

9 If the answer to question 8 is yes, do you ever try to hide this difference?

10 Are you a decisive person?

11 Do you ever criticise yourself for not being 'as good' as someone else?

12 You are an exception. Do you believe this?

13 Do you often wish that you looked like someone else?

14 Do you ever wish you *were* someone else?

15 If you are told that a rule applies to everyone and that there are no exceptions, do you automatically acquiesce?

16 Do you feel inspired by other people's successes?

17 If a friend buys a gorgeous designer item do you need to go out and buy something too?

18 Are you influenced by celebrity culture?

19 Would you describe yourself as your own person?

20 Do you relish new experiences?

Consider your answers and what they reveal about you. People who celebrate their uniqueness are more relaxed and confident than those who are forever trying to fit in.

There really is no such thing as the 'norm' or the 'average'. We have created such concepts in an attempt to categorise and structure our lives in some way but it is important to remember that standards and comparisons are not real measurements. There is no 'right' way of doing things, there is no 'normal' type or size of person (or bum!), and if you follow the herd you will never make an impact. People who stand out are those who dare to risk the censure of others; they are innovators and they shatter glass ceilings. When you dare to be different you challenge the status quo and you will inevitably infuriate someone or other. But unless you are prepared to give up on people-pleasing activities you will stay stuck in the rut of sameness.

It is impossible to recognise and appreciate your own intrinsic qualities if you are trying to be like someone else or you are afraid to rock the boat. But once you step forward and begin to celebrate your differences you will relax, let go and really start to be yourself. If you are confident then you make your own decisions, and you know your own values and stand by them. Follow your instincts and your creative urges and fulfil that incredible blueprint which is yours alone. You've got whatever it takes, so use it!

Enjoy yourself

We are naturally attracted to enthusiastic people. We are drawn to those who are having a great time and showing it because it reminds us that life is here to be relished and enjoyed, and that we can feel like this too. And on top of this we can also 'catch' the enthusiastic vibes of others; they rub off on us and we feel more inspired and creative. Who do you know who has this sort of passionate energy? Such a person will have a self-sufficiency about them; they are happy to spend time alone and they know how to enjoy their own company.

In the immortal words of John Donne, 'No man is an island, entire of itself.' And at a spiritual level this is indeed true: no man (or woman) is isolated because ultimately we are all connected. However, at an existential level we are always alone with our own thoughts and feelings.

INSTANT BOOST

FLAUNT YOUR DIFFERENCES

INSTEAD OF TRYING TO HIDE YOUR TOO LARGE BOTTOM, BIG NOSE, FRECKLES, UNMANAGEABLE HAIR, LOUD VOICE, SMALL BREASTS/LARGE BREASTS, TALL STATURE/SHORT STATURE . . . OR WHATEVER IT IS YOU WISH WAS MORE NORMAL AND ACCEPTABLE, CHOOSE TO MAKE A FEATURE OF IT.

TURN YOUR PERSONAL PREJUDICES AROUND AND INSTEAD OF BEING ASHAMED AND HIDING YOUR ORIGINALITY MAKE A DISPLAY OF IT. CONSIDER THE CHARISMATIC DAWN FRENCH (SIZE 20) WHO HAS BEEN VOTED THE PERSONALITY WHO HAS MOST INSPIRED BRITAIN'S YOUNGER WOMEN. IN A CULTURE OBSESSED WITH WEIGHT AND LOOKS DAWN HAS WON THROUGH WITH SHEER SELF-CONFIDENCE AND CHUTZPAH.

GO BACK TO YOUR FULL-LENGTH MIRROR AND PRACTISE FLAUNTING AND FLIRTING WITH YOUR IMAGE. GIVE IT ALL YOU'VE GOT AND THEN GO OUT INTO THE WORLD AND MAKE THE VERY MOST OF YOURSELF.

LEARN TO LOVE YOUR ORIGINALITY AND MAXIMISE WHATEVER YOU'VE GOT AND REMEMBER THAT SELF-CONFIDENCE IS ALLURING, BEGUILING AND CAPTIVATING. GET GOING!

Once you recognise your uniqueness you must also accept that you are on your own. No one can ever feel exactly what you are feeling or think what you are thinking. You can be listening to a band at a rock concert surrounded by thousands of others or be having amazingly intimate sex with another person or be by yourself in the bath; in every case you are alone with your own individual experience.

Meryl's story

When I met Meryl she was a social butterfly, surrounded by a great number of friends and colleagues. She worked in television production and was always flying off to the club or restaurant of the moment. She was in her thirties and had had numerous short-term affairs before meeting Michael. She came for coaching after Michael had ended their relationship.

At our first session I had to ask Meryl to turn off her mobile after it had rung six times in the first twenty minutes of our meeting. This obviously made her anxious and when I questioned her about this she said that she was always afraid to miss a call and that she needed to keep in constant contact with people.

Meryl was terrified of being on her own and so she made sure that she never was. She led an exhausting life crammed with work and social meetings and she never had a moment to herself until Michael left. He told her that he couldn't stand her 'neediness' and that he couldn't 'be there' for her 24/7 in the way she demanded. Meryl said that she didn't understand what he had meant by this because she had only wanted complete intimacy with him at all times because she adored him so much. She had also felt burdened with guilt because she often failed to understand him completely and thought this was her fault.

Now Michael had left she found it very difficult to go back to her flat at night and was staying up socialising into the early hours to avoid going home alone. One night she even picked up a guy who she didn't particularly fancy just so that she didn't have to sleep alone. It was at this point that she realised that she was in a state of crisis and needed to get a grip on her life. Meryl said that she didn't want to be 'alone in her head' and that she was always looking for someone to share her inner experiences. She was preoccupied by the fear of her own aloneness and said that sometimes when she realised that she was having her own thoughts and feelings and that no one else was aware of them it made her very afraid. Of course intimacy involves personal disclosure, this is how we get to close to people. But no one can ever know our private selves and although this might feel frightening it can also feel liberating.

I asked Meryl if she had *really* wanted Michael (or anyone else for that matter) to read her mind and she laughed and said 'probably not'. I suggested that she needed to change her attitude towards this existential dilemma. We are all alone and we have to come to terms with this. If we expect others to be with us physically, emotionally and mentally then we are asking for the impossible. The upside of this is that, while no one can totally know us and always 'be there' for us, we can't be expected to always be there for other people. Michael couldn't know her inner workings but then Meryl couldn't know his either. This meant that she was absolved of all the guilt she had felt about trying to totally understand him (and failing).

I suggested that Meryl began a journal and spent time with herself alone (with the phone off) making notes of her thoughts, feelings and experiences. This was a great hit as it formed a nightly focus and slowly helped her to spend time alone and enjoy it. I also recommended that she didn't rush into a new relationship but gave herself at least six months off to do her own thing. The journal work grew over the next few weeks and she began to think about creating new goals. Six months later she had taken a sabbatical and was planning a trip to Asia on her own. I was surprised by how quickly Meryl calmed down and began to get to know herself and enjoy her own company. Without her never-ending neediness she became self-assured and confident and ready to take charge of herself.

Enjoying yourself means enjoying 'you' and all that you are and can be. Once you can accept that your differences are what make you special and utterly unique then you can let your aloneness become a strength to you. The fact is that the people who make the biggest impact in life are those who rely on their own feelings and instincts; they do what they believe is right for them and they are not trying to be understood by others or to please them or to fit in to someone else's agenda.

You've got to be up for it

In other words, if you aren't focused on a goal you can never attain it.

- You will never get that great new job if you don't apply for it.
- You won't get that fabulous relationship if you keep putting up with second-rate men.
- You can't resolve financial problems unless you get it all down on paper and make a good realistic action plan.

INNER BOOST

MAKE A DATE WITH YOURSELF

TAKE YOURSELF OUT ON A JAUNT. DO SOMETHING THAT YOU LOVE RATHER THAN SOMETHING THAT YOU THINK YOU 'SHOULD' BE DOING. PERHAPS YOU COULD FIT IN A SPOT OF LUNCH AND JUST GIVE YOURSELF A GOOD TIME. HERE ARE SOME THINGS THAT CLIENTS HAVE DONE ON THEIR OWN:

- GONE TO THE THEATRE TO SEE A TOP SHOW
- TAKEN A WALK BY THE COAST AND HAD CHIPS IN NEWSPAPER ON THE PIER
- VISITED THE TATE MODERN AND SENT POSTCARDS TO FRIENDS
- FLEW TO PARIS FOR THE WEEKEND
- HAD A FIRST LESSON AT A DRY SKI SLOPE (THIS EVENTUALLY LED TO A GREAT WINTER HOLIDAY)
- HAD A MASSAGE AND REFLEXOLOGY TREATMENT
- WENT SHOPPING IN HARRODS, HAD LUNCH WITH A GLASS OF WINE, DID MORE SHOPPING
- WENT TO THE BALLET AT COVENT GARDEN
- READ A NOVEL IN THE PARK AND TOOK A CHAMPAGNE PICNIC
- BOOKED A DAY AT THE SANCTUARY FOR A FABULOUS PAMPERING EXPERIENCE.
- SPENT A DAY AT THE VICTORIA AND ALBERT MUSEUM
- WENT SHOPPING IN NEW YORK
- VISITED STRATFORD ON AVON AND SAW *A WINTER'S TALE*

- WENT ICE-SKATING FOR THE FIRST TIME
- WENT SWIMMING AND HAD A SAUNA AT A NEW HEALTH CLUB
- BOUGHT A TICKET FOR WIMBLEDON AND SAW TIM HENMAN PLAY
- HAD A HEAD MASSAGE AND THEN A NEW HAIRCUT AND HIGHLIGHTS
- RAN IN THE LONDON MARATHON (HAVING TRAINED FOR NINE MONTHS)
- WENT TO SEE PAUL MCCARTNEY PERFORM AT EARLS COURT

I HAVE NOTICED THAT ONCE CLIENTS START PLANNING DATES WITH THEMSELVES THEY HAVE SUCH A GOOD TIME THAT THEY GET MORE AND MORE ADVENTUROUS, AS YOU CAN SEE BY SOME OF THE TRIPS MENTIONED ON THIS LIST. START SMALL, DON'T DO ANYTHING THAT FEELS TOO MUCH FOR YOU AND STAY IN YOUR COMFORT ZONE TO ENSURE THAT YOU HAVE A GOOD TIME.

- You won't get fit and healthy if you don't watch what you eat and don't take enough exercise.
- You only create a great social life by getting out there and meeting people.

To make an impact on your life you must take assertive action. Everything changes but unless you direct the change you will never feel confident and in control. If you believe that 'things keep happening to me' then you will always feel like a puppet on a string, dancing to someone else's tune. If you feel victimised in any area of your life at the moment then remind yourself that *you* are the one who can make things happen for you; you have to be up for those great opportunities or they will pass you by.

The Dos and Don'ts of making and impact on your life

Do get noticed

If you are feeling shy then stop concentrating on yourself and direct your attention to others. This works like a dream every time. Confident people might be feeling nervous but they don't indulge this. Instead they use their adrenaline rushes to push their energy forward in a constructive way. Believe me, we *all* get nervous. If you could only see what goes on behind the scenes before a TV programme is filmed. People do the most bizarre things while they 'act out' their nerves. And then, when the camera rolls they look calm, poised and centred. Learn to use your 'nervous' energy rushes by thinking of them as power surges and use this power to your advantage.

Don't ever give up on yourself

When you are down, the very last thing you feel like doing is trying to make any sort of impact: you feel withdrawn and alone with your emotional pain and you just want to hide away. If this is how you are right now then let yourself go with this introverted energy. Rather than believing that you have no self-confidence, why not recognise that you are going through a hard time and give yourself some support? We are all so self-critical and as soon as we feel negative about ourselves we are inclined to beat ourselves up about it and get even more negative. Change this approach because it will never work for you. When you find yourself in that negative cycle of defeat make an impact on your day by loving and nurturing yourself. Instead of criticising yourself for being 'useless', 'lacking confidence' and being 'untogether' give yourself a good time. Treat yourself just the way you would treat your dearest friend when she feels low. When it all gets too much for me (yes, even life coaches get the blues!) I fill a hot water bottle and take to my bed and I stay there until the feeling passes. So do whatever it takes to be kind to yourself and you will make such a big impact on your mood.

Do your preparation

To be a success in life you must recognise the direct link between cause and effect. A winning outcome always depends on a well-prepared action plan. Perhaps you are thinking that some people just seem to get all the luck without having done any of the work. Next time you feel like this take a closer look and you are most likely to find that 'lucky breaks' usually come to those who have created their own good fortune through work, perseverance and focus. That 'new' best-selling author has probably been around for years and has written many other books before she hit the big time. The amazing 'unknown' singer who gets a great recording deal has usually spent years and years practising and refining her art. Rewards come to those who put in the effort; you create your own luck with single-minded vision, determination and good preparation. Take a clear look at your dream goal and then start activating it; one step at a time is the way to go.

Don't be afraid

What's your excuse for not going for the best? Are you: *too old, not clever enough, untalented, too busy, too fat, too* *tired . . .*etc.? Such negative self-beliefs have no meaning. If you want something in life then apply yourself to getting it. If you long to write then go on a creative writing course and find out how the publishing business works. If you would love to play the piano, get some lessons. If you have a great desire to go on the stage, sign up with your local drama group. It's so easy to go for your goals, you just have to start getting practical. The only thing standing in your way is yourself and all your lame excuses for not getting going. I know it can be daunting to look at a long-term goal; it can seem like an impossible dream, but it is not. All those 'reasons' that stop you going forward are only coming from your fear. Take heart, take courage and take this life and run with it. If you feel afraid then feel it and then get over yourself and get going. Don't ever limit yourself or you will live to regret it.

And if you are still prevaricating and pussy-footing around just spare a thought for Helen Keller, who proved that *nothing* can stand in the way of a person who is totally determined to make an impact.

Born in 1880, Helen contracted an illness before she was two years old, and she was left unable to see or hear. She never let these disabilities stand in her way; she went on to learn to communicate and to inspire millions of people through her spoken and written words. She travelled all over the world and became a leading public figure who campaigned on behalf of civil rights, human dignity, women's suffrage, and world peace. Let the following quote from Helen Keller be an inspiration to you:

They took away what should have been my eyes, but I remembered Milton's Paradise. They took away what should have been my ears, Beethoven came and wiped away my tears. They took away what should have been my tongue, but I had talked to God when I was young. He would not let them take away my soul – possessing that, I still possess the whole.

INNER REFLECTION

TOTAL RELAXATION

RELAX IN A QUIET PLACE, CLOSE YOUR EYES AND BECOME AWARE OF YOUR BREATHING. LET YOUR THOUGHTS DRIFT AWAY AS YOU BEGIN TO BREATHE IN A SENSE OF PEACE AND BREATHE OUT ALL PHYSICAL TENSION.

FOLLOW YOUR BREATHING: INHALING PEACE AND CALM AND EXHALING ALL STRESSES AND STRAINS.

AS YOU DROP INTO A QUIET AND CENTRED PLACE DEEP INSIDE, YOU CAN START TO BECOME AWARE OF YOUR BODY IN MORE DETAIL. NOW BEGIN TO SCAN YOUR BODY FOR ANY TENSION THAT YOU MIGHT BE HOLDING. START WITH YOUR FEET AND CHECK THEIR RELAXATION LEVELS. ARE YOU HOLDING ANY TENSION THERE? 1F SO, CONSCIOUSLY LET GO OF IT NOW. TRAVEL UP YOUR BODY SCANNING FOR TENSION AS YOU GO. AS YOU GET USED TO THIS PROCESS YOU WILL BEGIN TO BECOME VERY SENSITIVE TO YOUR BODILY FEELINGS, RECOGNISING THE REAL DIFFERENCES BETWEEN TENSION AND RELAXATION LEVELS.

WHEN YOU FEEL TENSION IN ANY PART OF YOUR BODY IMAGINE *BREATHING INTO* THE TENSION AND FEELING IT

MELT AWAY AS YOU BREATHE OUT. NOTICE HOW TENSION AND WORRIES BEGIN TO LOOSEN THEIR PHYSICAL GRIP ONCE YOU BEGIN TO RECOGNISE THEM. AS YOU WORK AT RELAXATION AT THE PHYSICAL LEVEL YOU WILL DISCOVER THAT YOU WILL BEGIN TO FEEL MUCH MORE MENTALLY RELAXED.

WHEN YOU ARE READY OPEN YOUR EYES AND SLOWLY COME BACK INTO THE ROOM. STAY WITH YOUR RELAXED FEELINGS AS LONG AS YOU CAN.

Be an Optimist

I've been on my knees many times, and the way I get out of it is looking at what I have. The exit for agony is always there, but you don't take it by choice.

The easiest way out is to say 'the grass is green and beautiful, the park is gorgeous, I saw a really pretty girl about five minutes ago, I had an interesting conversation with an old guy in the elevator . . . and I've got a frickin' excellent car!' If everyone did that before they went to bed at night, there would be no unhappy people!

JIM CARREY IN AN INTERVIEW FOR
NORTHERN WOMAN MAGAZINE

I know; he's rich and famous and can afford a 'frickin' excellent car', but Jim Carrey also knows a thing or two about being happy. In this interview to publicise his new film *Fun with Dick and Jane,* he goes on to explain how he keeps centred and calm amidst all the hype and artificiality of Hollywood.

'I am such a lucky human being. I have had a couple (of events) here and there that I have tried to blow up into something bigger, but for the most part it has just been a pretty amazing ride . . . To me, it is a matter of staying in a good place and realising what everything is really worth. I know we try to mythologise everything in Hollywood, so everything is blown out of proportion; but as far as I am concerned, I just make movies that make people feel good for, like, two hours. That is my thing I do in life and I'm OK with that – which is enough, I guess.'

The exit for agony *is* always there isn't it? But, as Jim Carrey suggests, we don't have to take that downhill negative path when we can choose a far easier and happier route. Oprah Winfrey takes a similar optimistic line when she suggests that, 'The more you praise and celebrate your life, the more there is in life to celebrate.'

If we can look at the grass and appreciate its greenness and beauty we feel uplifted. But if we think that the grass might be greener somewhere else then we will always feel dissatisfied. This reminds me of my early days at university when we freshers would spend all night trailing round the campus bars and any party that might be going, in a never-ending search for 'where it was at'. We were never able to enjoy any event to the full for fear that we might be missing something better somewhere else. And this brings me to one of the major talents of the optimist: she knows how to celebrate the simple things in life and how to appreciate and value who she is and what she has. This might sound a very simplistic approach but it is actually at the very heart of Positive Psychology.

Martin Seligman is a cognitive psychologist, who is a leading light in the Positive Psychology movement and has spent years clinically testing the concept of 'learned help-lessness'. He gave mild electric shocks to dogs and proved that most of them would give up trying to escape if they believed that the shocks would keep on coming. Another researcher tested this principle on people, using noise to replace shocks, and discovered that the condition of learned helplessness can be just as easily produced in human minds. But the experiments contained a fascinating anomaly. Just as Seligman found in the dog experiments, one in every three human subjects refused to 'give up' and kept trying to press buttons on a panel in order to stop the noise. What made these people so persistent? How did they differ from the others?

When he applied these questions to real-life situations, Seligman discovered that those who could bounce back from adversity had a different outlook on life than those who gave up in defeat. These people had developed a positive way of explaining and understanding events; they had learned the skills of optimism.

INSTANT BOOST

YOU ARE AN OPTIMIST

YOU MIGHT NOT THINK THAT YOU ARE BUT YOU ARE! HOW ELSE HAVE YOU MANAGED TO KEEP GOING WITH A SMILE ON YOUR FACE? AND WHY DID YOU BUY THIS BOOK? YOU BOUGHT IT BECAUSE YOU KNOW THAT YOU CAN CHANGE YOUR MIND-SET. PESSIMISTS ARE CYNICAL ABOUT SELF-HELP BECAUSE THEY DON'T BELIEVE THAT THEY HAVE ANY POWER. YOU KNOW THAT YOU HAVE THE POWER AND THIS GIVES YOU AN ENORMOUS HEAD START. EVEN IF YOU ARE NOT FEELING POSITIVE AT THE MOMENT, TAKE THIS CHANCE TO REMEMBER A TIME WHEN YOU BOUNCED BACK FROM HARD TIMES.

THE DIFFICULT SITUATION I FACED WAS . . . .

AT THE TIME I WAS FEELING . . . .

AND I WAS THINKING . . . .

I FACED THE CHALLENGE WHEN I . . . .

AFTERWARDS I FELT . . . .

I DISCOVERED THE FOLLOWING INNER STRENGTHS . . . . .

. . . .

NOTICE THAT THESE STRENGTHS ARE THE QUALITIES OF AN
OPTIMIST. REMIND YOURSELF OF THESE QUALITIES WHEN-
EVER YOU ARE FEELING NEGATIVE. YOU SEE YOU REALLY
DO KNOW HOW TO BE OPTIMISTIC; IT'S ONLY A THOUGHT
AWAY.

Remember to be positive

Dr Nick Baylis is Lecturer in Positive Psychology at
Cambridge University and he writes an uplifting weekly
column in one of Britain's broadsheet magazines. He writes
under the name of Dr Feelgood and I just love his optimistic
and empowering approach.

Writing about the benefits of savouring one's blessings he
says that, '. . . encouraging our wellbeing requires us not
merely to reduce our negative practices, but to actively
pursue our life-enhancing ones . . . Our psychological health
is not so much a reflection of what we do wrong, so much as
what we do right.' He goes on to suggest that we take a few
five-minute breaks throughout our day in order to 'cherry-
pick some pleasures'.

Try this right now. Put down the book and look back over
your day. What have you particularly appreciated? Perhaps
you had a great enlivening phone call or maybe you enjoyed

feeling the sun on your face as you walked to work. Use such small memories at various times in the day to keep you hooked into positive experiences and a positive mood. You could use the same technique whenever you feel yourself slipping into a negative state so that you literally 'pull' your energy back into the positive cycle. Notice how this pulling effect feels, and visualise yourself radiating charisma.

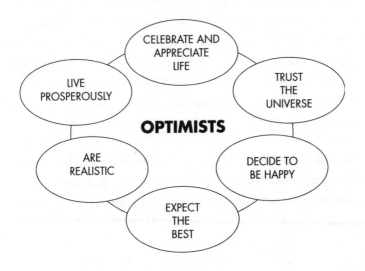

OPTIMISTS

Optimism is . . .

Trusting the universe
Many years ago, when I was a single mum with two very young children I hit a real low point. I felt stuck at every level and didn't know which way to turn. Until then I had always

been a pretty upbeat person but I could feel myself going further and further down and I had no hope for the future. And then I discovered Louise Hay's book *You Can Heal Your Life*. Of course this book is now a classic but back then it was considered a rather whacky American self-help book (the genre was then in its infancy).

I remember lying in bed one night and reading that, 'The Universe totally supports us in every thought we choose to think and believe.' Louise then went on to clarify this by saying, 'Put another way, our subconscious mind accepts whatever we choose to believe.' This meant that whatever I believed about my world and myself would become true for me in some way; I created my reality with my belief system and my beliefs could be changed.

From that night I was a changed woman. Suddenly everything made sense to me and I started saying affirmations in earnest. I wore out my first copy of Louise's book; it fell apart eventually and I had to buy another. By that time I had indeed healed my life and in fact had written my own self-help book, *Creating Self-Esteem*, and when it was published Louise Hay sent me a handmade congratulations card. I had learned to trust the universe by understanding that I was creating my own experiences, and this is surely the most empowering realisation of all.

If you are finding it hard to see the benevolence of the universe at the moment, try repeating the following affirmation taken from *You Can Heal Your Life*:

In the infinity of life where I am,
all is perfect, whole and complete.
The past has no power over me
because I am willing to learn and to change.

Optimists expect the best possible outcome because they believe in themselves and their ability to change their life.

Deciding to be happy

Yes, we really do have this choice and sometimes people get very irritated when I remind them of this. But happiness really is a state of mind (as is sadness) and the optimists of the world have learned how to cultivate this positive quality. Happiness is a response to what is happening to you and you can create this feeling whenever you wish.

Expecting the best

The pessimist's philosophy is bound up in the fear of disappointment. Think back to a time when you were afraid to expect the best. What did you do? Did you expect the worst? What happened? Were your worst fears realised?

Because we know that our expectations help to create our outcome, we are always better off backing the optimistic horse. The Eeyores of the world moan and complain and take their pleasure when they can say, 'I knew it would be a disaster' (or words to that effect). The Tiggers of the world bounce along in hopeful expectancy; but notice that they bounce rather than moan. Yes, sometimes we optimists are disappointed but remember that pessimists are disappointed *all* the time. Next time you face the choice of being hopeful or despondent why not try the hopeful positive path? You will attract positive energy into the situation, plus you will feel great. Cynics feel like losers and optimists feel like winners; *you* choose what to expect!

True optimists are not foolish people with their head in the clouds who are continually banging on about 'keeping positive' and 'looking on the bright side of life'. Various pessimists that I have met along the way seem to have a jaundiced view of the power of positivity (but of course they would, wouldn't they?). I have learned not to react to this view and in fact I let it work for me. When people start to get negative around me I become *even more positive*. It works like a dream because positive vibrations are just much more powerful than negative ones and in the end the pessimists just have to give up.

EXERCISE:

Be a realist

Optimists are realistic people who support their positive vision with appropriate action. They do this by:

- Having positive thoughts
- Creating a positive vision
- Doing whatever needs to be done

Take any situation you find yourself in at the moment. Now what would be the most positive approach that you could take? Find out by completing the following sentences.

My positive thoughts about this are ....
I visualise a positive outcome by imagining ....
I will take the following positive action ....
I will take this action by (specify a date) ....

When your thoughts, visions and actions match each other you are bound to have a successful outcome. Optimists know that they will never lose, because even if things don't turn out exactly as they had planned, they have given it their best shot and couldn't have done any more.

Sometimes the universe has a different plan for us than the one we had imagined and very often (with hindsight) we can see why. So keep trusting yourself, trust the universe and stay optimistic.

You get what you expect

Clients often come for coaching without a particular personal goal in mind. They may feel stuck and unclear about which way to turn and want to get some clarity into their life. This is a perfectly valid expectation although sometimes people are a bit embarrassed to admit that they are uncertain and undecided. But this feeling of stuckness or dissatisfaction with how things are is a natural and cyclical event for every one of us. Life is always changing and we are part of that change. A relationship that was once brilliant might not be right any more. A career path that felt good five years ago might now need reassessing. Perhaps we are just feeling in a rut and don't know how to climb out of it.

When someone tells me that they are miserable or fed-up I reinterpret these messages and refer to them as points of divine discontent. In this way we get to look at our unhappiness in an optimistic rather than a pessimistic light. I take the view that our dissatisfaction holds the key to the changes that we need to make, and this is why it is called divine! The universe sends us the very lessons we need in order to develop and achieve our potential. Reflect on what the universe is sending to you right now. Where do you need to change something?

Kate's story

Kate, 29, is a teacher and she shares a flat with Liz, 32, who is an accountant. Kate and Liz are like chalk and cheese, or so Kate would have me believe. They had been friends for a few years but once they started living together Kate became more and more depressed. When she came for coaching she told me that she was beginning to hate Liz because she was always so happy and popular and that she (Kate) felt like such a sourpuss in comparison. Kate wanted to feel happier, brighter and more positive about life; she wanted some of that optimistic and upbeat energy that Liz had.

Liz sounded like a girl with a kind heart who kept as positive as she could and had a lighthearted approach, which made her socially attractive, and basically Kate was jealous of her. It took a few weeks for all this to reveal itself because Kate was embarrassed and ashamed of her feelings. But as soon as she came clean she felt much better and went on to tell me about her parents.

Her mother and father were never the types to be the life and soul of the party and growing up with them was quite a sombre affair. Kate was their only child and they were both people who were pessimistic and negative by inclination. They had struggled in their own childhoods and both of them were what Kate described as 'disappointed people' who were always ready for the worst to happen. As she talked more about them Kate began to realise that they had actually been trying to protect her from disappointment and failure by teaching her to never expect anything good to happen. Their fear of being disappointed had been passed on to Kate who had become a 'permanent pessimist' (her words).

Once Kate had made this important connection and

recognised how her negative beliefs were holding her back she became transformed. In fact she reminded me of myself when I first realised that our beliefs create our world and that we can change them so that they support us. She went on to work hard with positive affirmations and used many of the tips I have written about in this book. She is now a new woman who has learned the skills of the optimist. At our last meeting she told me that her relationship with Liz had been an amazing catalyst that had brought her for coaching and changed her completely.

INNER REFLECTION

ARE YOU DIVINELY DISCONTENTED?

CHECK YOUR OWN AREAS OF DISSATISFACTION AND LOOK CLOSELY TO SEE WHAT MESSAGES LIE THERE FOR YOU.

- CHOOSE ANY AREA OF YOUR LIFE WHERE YOU ARE FEELING STUCK, IRRITATED, ANNOYED OR LESS THAN HAPPY.
- NAME YOUR GRIEVANCES.
- DID YOU PLAY ANY PART IN CREATING THIS DISCONTENT?
- IF SO WHAT DID YOU DO?
- HOW CAN YOU INSTIGATE THE CHANGES YOU WANT TO SEE?
- WHAT CAN YOU LEARN ABOUT YOURSELF FROM THIS SITUATION?

IMAGINE THAT THE UNIVERSE IS SENDING YOU GUIDANCE; WHAT IS IT TRYING TO TELL YOU ABOUT YOURSELF?

Live richly and prosperously

Optimists feel prosperous whether they are rich or poor because prosperity is a state of mind that embraces the abundance of the universe and trusts in its benevolence. We all know miserable and grumpy people who are well off; they might have wealth but it doesn't necessarily bring them happiness. And I'm sure you know others who might not be rich in money but who have a sunny aspect and know how to enjoy the good things in life and share in its bounty.

If you are feeling needy it's because you are not getting enough of whatever you want, whether it's confidence, respect, attention, love, money or whatever. It is very easy to blame a lack of money when you are feeling a lack of resources, but actually scarcity consciousness and a negative fear-based attitude will create an aura of 'poor energy' around you, and it is *this* that attracts a sense of deficiency into your life. Poor energy attracts scarcity and rich energy attracts prosperity. When you feel prosperous you are generous, open-hearted and sensitive to others. These qualities are extremely attractive and draw towards you the most positive outcomes that you could imagine. Optimists carry an air of 'rich energy' about them because they are always looking for the constructive aspect rather than the negative one, and they affirm a positive worldview. Pessimists perpetuate an air of doom and gloom and affirm a negative worldview. They choose to focus on lack and scarcity and their 'poor energy' makes them very unattractive to others.

Consider the optimists and pessimists that you know. How does their 'rich' or 'poor' energy affect their relationship with you? Notice how an optimist always leaves you feeling more confident about yourself and life in general and how a pessimist just drains away your positive feelings.

Checking your worldview

What have you learned to believe about the world and its inhabitants? Put 'I believe that. . .' before each of the following statements and answer yes or no. Don't spend too long deliberating, just go with your first instinct.

                                                                      Yes No

1 The more I give the less I have.

2 We have the power to change the world.

3 My contribution counts.

4 Our natural resources are limited.

5 My life is an amazing experience.

6 I can change my reality.

7 We are all connected.

8 I am insignificant in the grand scheme of things.

9 Life is a celebration.

10 This is a world of plenty.

11 We are here to take care of each other.

12 Events are beyond my control.

13 I can change my reality.

14 We are naturally creative and loving.

15 The world is a dangerous place.

Reading through your answers, you might be surprised to discover that you are indulging in scarcity consciousness without even being aware of it. We know how our negative self-beliefs can stand in our way and similarly so can our beliefs about the universe. If you believe that the world offers limited gifts and that there is 'not enough' of anything to go round and that we are competing with each other for limited resources then you are focusing on lack and carrying poor energy in your aura. Such an attitude actually *creates* limitation. A feeling of scarcity brings with it fear, greed, competitiveness, aggression and a betrayal of the natural laws.

The fabulous truth is that *the universe is abundant: it has everything we need.* Our world is naturally prolific: there is no shortage unless we have created it. There is enough food if we work with the balance of nature and for the good of all; there is enough air, unless we decide to pollute it; there is enough love if we choose to radiate it; there is enough of everything if we believe there is and then act in harmony with those beliefs. Still wondering if this is true? Go out and look for abundance and you will see it everywhere. Check out the proliferation of tadpoles in your pond, the blades of grass in the park, the number of apples on the tree. Try counting the seeds in your tomato, the stars in the sky or the smiles on your baby's face.

Scarcity is an idea that only becomes a reality if we believe in it. Refuse to buy into this concept. Embrace abundance in all its generous forms, seek it out and focus on what there is rather than on what there isn't. Think abundantly; live prosperously, keep optimistic and surround yourself with the richness and wonder of the universe.

And when you take your 'abundant' beliefs out into the world an amazing thing happens: you create win–win situations wherever you go. Because you know that there is plenty of everything to go round you have no need to compete with others; in fact you know that cooperation is always the key to real achievement. For one person to succeed it does not necessarily

follow that another must fail. And this leads to you searching for
solutions to problems that allow everyone involved to benefit.

When you are able to make people around you feel like
winners you inspire confidence and support, which of course
leads on to further positive outcomes.

---

10 Good reasons to hold a positive worldview

1 Your levels of self-esteem and self-worth rise as you learn
   to trust the universe.
2 You feel good and look good because you are so much
   happier.
3 These feel-good qualities rub off on to all the people that
   you meet.
4 It is an expansive state as it attracts all other forms of
   positivity.
5 Stress levels fall as you drop your fearful attitude.
6 You realise that you can create your own reality because
   positive thoughts are an agent for conscious change.
7 It gets easier and easier to take the optimistic path when
   you know that everything supports your powerful
   intention to succeed.
8 Each day becomes an exciting adventure because
   anything feels possible.
9 You become hugely attractive to others because you
   walk, talk and act with confidence.
10 When you start to really appreciate your life it becomes
   more and more precious and meaningful.

INSTANT BOOST

RISE TO THE CHALLENGE

THE WORDS WE USE MAKE A BIG DIFFERENCE TO OUR PERCEPTIONS. IT IS NOTICEABLE THAT THOSE WHO ARE INCLINED TO PESSIMISM OFTEN USE NEGATIVE WORDS AND EXPRESSIONS (E.G. REFERRING TO DIFFICULT SITUATIONS AS 'PROBLEMS' OR STARTING SENTENCES WITH THE PHRASE 'THE TROUBLE IS'). WHEN WE USE SUCH WORDS OUR ENERGY ACTUALLY DROPS AND TAKES US INTO FURTHER NEGATIVITY. SO WATCH THE WORDS YOU USE. KEEP YOUR ENERGY UPBEAT AND OPTIMISTIC BY TAKING A NEW LOOK AT YOUR SO-CALLED 'PROBLEMS'.

- BRING TO MIND AN ONGOING DIFFICULTY (NOTICE HOW YOUR ENERGY DROPS AT THE MERE THOUGHT OF IT).
- NOW WRITE A BRIEF, FACTUAL DESCRIPTION OF YOUR SITUATION; BE AS OBJECTIVE AS POSSIBLE.
- BE AWARE OF YOUR LEVEL OF ENERGY AND CONCENTRATE ON STOPPING IT FALLING.
- DECIDE TO VIEW YOUR 'PROBLEM' AS A 'CHALLENGE' AND NOTICE HOW THE DIFFERENT TERMS EXTRACT A DIFFERENT ENERGETIC RESPONSE FROM YOU.

THE WORD 'PROBLEM' BRINGS WITH IT IMAGES OF OBSTACLES AND LIMITS; NO WONDER WE FEEL DAUNTED AT THE VERY MENTION OF THE WORD. HOWEVER, WE CAN ALWAYS 'RISE TO' AND OVERCOME A CHALLENGE, CAN'T WE? SO CAN YOU RISE TO THIS PARTICULAR CHALLENGE OF YOURS?

ALL YOU NEED TO DO IS: TO *RECOGNISE* WHY YOU HAVE ATTRACTED THIS CHALLENGE, TO *UNDERSTAND* WHY YOU CONTINUE TO DO THIS AND TO *CHANGE* YOUR ENERGETIC PATTERNS SO THAT YOU CAN MOVE ON.

RECOGNISING / *UNDERSTANDING* / *CHANGING* IS THE PROCESS WE USE WHEN WE TAKE A POSITIVE APPROACH TO OVERCOMING OUR PERSONAL OBSTACLES. THE OPTIMIST KNOWS THAT THERE IS NOTHING STANDING IN HER WAY THAT SHE CANNOT STEP OVER.

You have to be in it to win it

And being in it requires that you openly declare your interest and put yourself out there. You will notice that pessimists rarely stake their claim in this way, preferring to keep a low profile and hold back on their dreams for fear of failure.

Ellen MacArthur is a woman of spirit, talent, courage, determination and optimism. When she completed her single-handed round the world voyage in record-breaking time in 2005, she beat the mark set by Francis Joyon. After her awesome achievement the yachtswoman said, 'I always believed that I could break the record, and Francis agreed it was breakable. But I really didn't think that I would do it at the first attempt.'

Dame Ellen first caught the public eye in 2001 when she finished second in the Vendée Globe, the toughest single-handed circumnavigation of the globe by yacht. She was the youngest and smallest competitor as well as being the only woman. Talking about what keeps her going, alone at sea, she said that the sailor's preservation system 'makes you forget just how bad things are – otherwise, you would be in too much shock. And it's that which allows you to go back out there and do it again.' Well, whatever she calls it, it obviously works for her, but I rather think that this 'system' actually stems from Ellen's own personal tenacity and sheer self-belief and personal grit.

She says that her biggest fear is 'probably failure' and that she was inspired to rise to the challenge when she came last in all the races at sailing school when she was ten. 'On the journey home I decided that I would never let that happen again,' she recalled. 'I wasn't going to be last, no matter what it took.' How interesting that her fear of failure inspired her to greatness rather than terrifying her into giving up.

Ellen has all the qualities of a winner and we must admire her optimistic and confident approach to the realisation of her sporting dreams. She risked failure and overcame hardship and loneliness in her quest to break Joyon's record but she felt the fear and did it anyway. You can never 'win it' if you are never 'in it'; step forward into your life and go for your own dreams. And in the words of Ellen MacArthur remember that:

There will be very difficult days but you deal with it – that's what makes the experience richer.

EXERCISE:

Visualising abundance

Relax in a comfortable position and read the following passage.

You can hear a bird singing in the distance, its song is

beautiful and clear. You can hear the bird getting closer and you look up and see a fantastic bird of paradise. It has feathers of every imaginable colour: red, blue, green, yellow, orange, purple and pink. It looks like a bright jewel. The bird calls to you as it flies ahead and you follow. When you look around you find yourself in a buttercup meadow. The sky is very blue, the grass is a beautiful green and there are buttercups everywhere, their golden cups bobbing in the light breeze. You are following a narrow path and ahead you can see some cows grazing in the distance. You have a feeling of great peace. The warm golden sun is caressing your skin and you can hear the mooing of the cows and the buzzing of the bees. This is a beautiful and safe place. The bird has stopped ahead and is sitting on a branch of a large, leafy oak tree. You sit down on the grass and lean back against the trunk of the tree.

The air is fragrant with the smells of freshly mown grass, honeysuckle and lavender. You rest there in the sunshine, enjoying the beautiful place and feeling deeply contented.

You can hear the gentle trickle of water flowing nearby and you notice a small stream running alongside the path. You see brightly coloured fish swimming in the clear water and dragonflies with their bejewelled wings of blues and greens hovering over the surface.

The bird flies on ahead and, feeling well rested, you follow. Soon you realise that your path is winding upwards towards the source of the stream at the top of the hill, and there, where the stream begins, you see a white castle shining in the sunshine. It is exquisite and looks just like something from a fairytale. You feel excited and follow the bird to the entrance.

As you climb the steps of the castle you hear the sounds of beautiful music and laughter. There is a party going on inside. You know that you are welcome. In fact you know that everyone is waiting for you. As you enter everybody turns to smile at you. Every person you have ever met is here. There is your family and loved ones, there are your friends, there are your acquaintances, there are the people you don't like, there are your enemies . . . Look around at everyone, they are all smiling at you with their arms outstretched in welcome. You hear them say together, 'We have all been waiting for you. You are very welcome here.'

Your heart feels full of joy and happiness. Wander around the castle and enjoy the hospitality . . . There is an abundance of everything, more than plenty for everyone.

Then you see the bird again. It flies ahead and indicates that you follow. You climb the winding staircase to the very top floor and here you discover a huge roomful of treasures. Look at the jewels, the beautiful clothes, the gold and silver and enjoy the opulence; there is just so much of everything. The bird asks you to take a gift from the room; you can have anything you like. Choose your gift. Now you leave the treasure chamber and go back down the stairs, passing all the familiar faces. People are shaking your hand or hugging you as they say their goodbyes. You feel very warm and close towards everyone. As you reach the castle entrance you turn for one last look. Everyone is smiling at you as they say together, 'Come back whenever you wish. We will always be here.' You are feeling contented and happy as you step from the castle into the bright warm sunshine.

The bird flies ahead as you take the winding path to the bottom of the hill. You walk slowly alongside the stream carrying your gift from the castle, until you reach the oak tree where you rest against the trunk again. Look around at the golden buttercups. See the cows in the distance. Smell the grass, the lavender and the honeysuckle. This is a beautiful and tranquil place and you feel safe and happy. You know that you can always come here to rest and become refreshed. Everyone whom you have ever met will always be here to welcome you whenever you wish to return.

You know now that your journey is over. You are ready to go home happy and contented. Return slowly. Rub your hands together, stretch and feel yourself coming back into your body.

When you have read through the instructions a couple of times you will be ready to create the visualisation for yourself. Relax completely and this time close your eyes and take yourself on the journey. Give yourself plenty of time to enjoy all your experiences along the way.

You can recreate this experience in a moment by imagining that you are holding the gift that you brought back from the castle. When you hold your treasure you are reminded of the feelings that you experienced in the beautiful place of your vision. You feel safe, contented, peaceful, relaxed, happy and loved: you experience the abundance of our universe.

INNER REFLECTION

SMILE UPON AWAKENING

In *The Miracle of Mindfulness,* Thich Nhat Hanh reminds us of the very best way to begin our day. He says, 'Hang a branch, any other sign, or even the word "smile" on the ceiling or wall so that you see it right away when you open your eyes. This sign will serve as your reminder.'

Yes, this is a good way to start the day, every day. As you open your eyes each morning, just smile and feel yourself becoming relaxed and centred. Take this quiet time to reflect upon the promise of the day ahead and feel your smiling thoughts going out into the world to attract positive and prosperous outcomes.

Notice the effect that such a start has on the rest of your day. Your smiling awareness concentrates your mind and emotions in a positive and appreciative way, which leaves no room for worry and negative pre-occupations.

Begin every day in this way, and let this simple meditation become part of your waking-up routine. It won't be long before you begin to feel the amazing impact that this has on the quality of your life.

Smile and expect the best

Go with the Flow

I believe we must find, all of us together, a new Spirituality. This new concept ought to be elaborated alongside the religions in such a way that all people of good will could adhere to it.

HIS HOLINESS THE DALAI LAMA

While many people are happy to examine and discuss their thoughts and behaviour they often find it much harder to talk about their emotions. And you will have noticed that men usually find this even more difficult than women. Those of us who haven't had much practice at sharing our feelings might be suffering from a condition called emotional illiteracy, whereby we are limited by a lack of useful vocabulary. We can't acknowledge our feelings because we just don't have the words to describe them adequately. I am happy to say that this situation is beginning to improve as counselling, life coaching and self-help have become mainstream activities and more and more people recognise that it is good for our emotional health to share our feelings with others. But as we become more emotionally literate it is noticeable that we are now struggling to find the words to express our spiritual awareness.

Our spirituality is such an important part of who we are that it's vitally important that we have the language to discuss it. But spiritual literacy is still in its infancy with many clients feeling unsure about what the word 'spiritual' actually means. Don't confuse spirituality with religion; they are not necessarily connected. Your spiritual energy gives you your love and passion for life. It speaks to you through your intuition and imagination and can bring you a wonderful sense of meaning, purpose and peace.

Holistic life coaching

The energy of the universe is naturally balanced and freely flowing unless it becomes blocked in some way by human interference. As we are part of this cosmic whole, our energy also flows freely unless this process becomes obstructed. When we are feeling confident, optimistic, centred and purposeful there is nothing that we cannot achieve; we can realise our true potential when we integrate all our energies in a balanced and harmonious way and we go with the flow.

I take a holistic approach with my clients, which means that I relate to the energy of the 'whole' person. Simply put, this means that human beings exist simultaneously at the spiritual, mental, emotional and physical levels and so we bring all four aspects of our humanness to each of our experiences. The diagram opposite shows how this works.

We understand and interpret our lives through our mind, body, spirit and emotions. Our mental, physical, spiritual and emotional energies are subtle, interwoven and mutually dependent; they colour and shape each other. For example, how we feel affects what we do, and if we change our emotion our actions may also change. Similarly, if we change our behaviour we often feel completely different. And over and over again we have seen how our thinking impacts on

SPIRITUAL

PHYSICAL

A TOTAL EXPERIENCE

MENTAL

EMOTIONAL

A TOTAL EXPERIENCE

our whole lives; for example, positive thoughts create emotional, mental and spiritual wellbeing. Our energies are always connected and when they are flowing smoothly our total experience is complete and we feel confident and in control and in touch with what is going on. If there is an imbalance anywhere we will experience the knock-on effects in every part of ourselves and we will feel disconnected, out of sorts, uneasy and low in confidence.

Whether I am working with a group or on a one-to-one basis, I am always aware of the subtle interplay of energies. The balance is important because we can only make positive change when our whole being is focused and centred. Once clients can recognise and understand their personal imbalances we can really get going and do some good work together. But you can do this for yourself. Just take a look at the following table and you will see the different experiences we have with our different types of energy.

Type of energy		Type of experience
Spiritual	➤	Connecting with life force (inner awareness)
Mental	➤	Understanding
Emotional	➤	Feeling
Physical	➤	Action

Imagine that you and I are meeting. You bring your spiritual, mental, emotional and physical energy to this encounter. You bring a spiritual experience of your own inner awareness, your *connection* with the life force. You *understand* the encounter with your mental energy. Your emotional energy allows you to *have feelings* about what is going on and your physical energy enables you to play an *active* part in the interaction. Can you see how these elements would come together to create the total experience for you?

Of course these 'types' of energy are not really separate; they affect each other so that all our experiences are multi-dimensional. When your energies are balanced your *connecting, understanding, feeling* and *acting* combine to create a confident and upbeat experience. But if you cannot smoothly integrate your energies you will feel less than your best and life will feel like an uphill climb.

Whenever your life feels 'stuck' it means that you need to shift some energy somewhere to get things going again. You know how this feels; it's like wearing heavy boots in a river of treacle and every step is a massive effort. Actually, this feeling can be very depressing and leads directly into the negative cycle of defeat. But look at it in another way.

If you feel stuck then there is a block in the flow of your energy and all you need do is find out where the imbalance lies.

What 'type' of person are you?

Of course you experience life with all of your energy. But until you have learned to balance your mind, body, spirit and emotions you will probably find that you often fall into one of the categories below.

Mental

You might be a cerebral person, who is very good at *understanding* ideas and following concepts but finds it hard to act spontaneously and be practical when it is necessary. Intellectual types also sometimes struggle to have experiences beyond those of the mind (difficulty in *connecting and feeling*).

Emotional

Or maybe you are the sort of person who is very sensitive to other people's *feelings*; you are emotionally aware and in touch with your own *feelings*, but does this gift sometimes cause you difficulties? Are you able to stop yourself from becoming so overwhelmed by your emotions that you are unable to *act*?

Physical

On the other hand you may be good at *action* and can be counted upon to be practical in any situation, but you have little concept of anything beyond that which you can see in front of you. In other words, you are a person who believes that 'seeing is believing'. If this is the case then you are having difficulty in *connecting*.

Spiritual

Perhaps you are someone who can easily reflect on her 'inner life' and knows how to relax but struggles to bring this experience into material reality. In other words, you can *connect* but can't easily *act* upon this connection; you have an inspired imagination but you find it hard to put this into effect.

Find the balance

When life feels good and you are motivated, confident and enthusiastic you know that your energies are balanced and flowing freely (you are in the flow). And when the feel-good factor is missing from your life you know that you are experiencing an imbalance somewhere. Although our four 'types' of energy are interdependent it is often very useful to look at each of them separately, to find out exactly where the difficulty might lie. Run through this personal checklist whenever you need to get yourself back in the flow.

Ask yourself these questions:

- Am I in touch with my mental energy? Am I just reacting to a series of 'musts', 'oughts' and 'shoulds'? Do I look at life through a negative filter?
- Am I taking care of my emotional energy? Can I accept and express my feelings or am I in denial over something?

- Am I behaving assertively and taking responsibility for my actions or am I acting like a victim?
- Am I in touch with my spiritual energy? Do I connect with my inner awareness or am I 'doing' too much and 'being' too little?

In my experience people can deal with imbalances in their mental, physical and emotional energies more easily than they can address a spiritual imbalance. They can look at their beliefs and begin changing them; work on getting in touch with their feelings and start to express them; and check out their behaviour to see if their actions support their highest needs, but they are often daunted about where to start on the spiritual front.

People are sometimes anxious when I use the word 'spiritual', asking such questions as: Is it anything to do with religion? Do you have to believe in God? Is it anything to do with cults? Does it mean behaving differently and meditating for hours? Do you have to eat lentils and muesli? Will I have to stop playing in a band, dyeing my hair and going to the pub? Have no fear; increasing your spiritual awareness will not necessarily make demands on you to change your lifestyle. It will only ever be a positive influence, because it increases the quality and depth of all your experiences.

Remember, it's a wonderful life

There can be no doubt that Frank Capra's *It's a Wonderful Life* is one of today's most popular Christmas films, which is quite amazing as it was made in 1946. I am sure you know the film but if you don't then see if you can rent it from a video shop.

This emotionally uplifting, feel-good movie stars James Stewart as George, the unsung, beloved hero of the small town of Bedford Falls. Throughout his life George had always placed human need above riches and as a result his only wealth was in his friends and family. When mounting personal and financial problems plunge him into the deepest despair and thoughts of suicide, his guardian angel Clarence is sent to prove to George that his life is worth living.

Clarence grants George a wish: to see what the world would be like if he hadn't been born. They travel together through the terrible alternative reality and see how much worse off many people would be. In the end George realises the value of his life and the importance of his personal contribution, and it is this message that has us weeping into our Kleenex at every Christmas re-run of this film.

Your life is important; your contribution is significant, but maybe you need reminding of this spiritual truth.

EXERCISE:

The difference you make

- What is different because you are alive? List at least ten things . . . .

- What is the most surprising item on your list? . . . .

- Why does this surprise you? . . . .

- What does this demonstrate about the type of person that you are? . . . .

This is such a good little exercise to do when you are feeling at a bit of a loss. We can get so distracted by the material world and the ways that 'success' is usually valued, that we lose sight of what is really important. When you reflect on the important differences that you make to the world you tap into your own emotional and spiritual strengths. Never forget that you are living a wonderful life!

INNER REFLECTION

REASONS TO BE HAPPY

SMILE AND RELAX AND GIVE THANKS FOR YOUR DAY. YOU HAVE SO MANY REASONS TO BE HAPPY. FOCUS ON THESE THINGS RIGHT NOW.

CLOSE YOUR EYES AND FOLLOW YOUR BREATHING UNTIL YOUR MIND AND BODY ARE QUIET.

IMAGINE THAT YOU ARE SITTING IN A CIRCLE WITH ALL YOUR LOVED ONES. LOOK AT EVERY PERSON IN TURN AND OPEN YOUR HEART TO EACH OF THEM.

SILENTLY THANK EACH ONE FOR THE BLESSINGS THEY BRING TO YOUR LIFE.

BE GRATEFUL FOR ALL YOU HAVE AND TAKE TIME EACH DAY TO GIVE THANKS.

Clouds of glory

Retail therapy can do wonders for a flagging ego and certainly I can shop 'til I drop like the best of them. But however much I love that designer suit or great pair of heels I know that my emotional rewards are only transient; the material world cannot give me everything I seek. And I know that you know this too. We want to have our cake and eat it, and why not indeed? We want to look fabulous on the outside *and* feel amazing on the inside: we need access to great shops *and* need a sense of meaning and purpose in our lives. Think of it like this: we must balance our material desires with our spiritual awareness, and inner peace comes from getting this balance right.

If we are not spiritually connected in any way then we will begin to feel that there is something missing in our lives and this can begin to dominate our days, leaving a sense of discontent and unhappiness with our lot. When we feel like this no amount of shopping will fill the emptiness; no amount of chocolate will do the trick; no object that we can buy will give us the satisfaction that we seek. If you have ever had the thought that 'there must be more to life than this' then you are quite right; there is!

Your inner world creates your outer world. This means that if you are at peace with yourself and enjoy the abundance of the universe then you will attract good, supportive relationships and positive outcomes. On the other hand if you are in inner turmoil you will find yourself at odds with others and you will draw negative people and circumstances into your orbit. Your humanness means that you are naturally spiritual. Universal energy is flowing through you and everyone else, and we are all connected to that divine spark of consciousness that gives us life. Stop looking for external examples of your spirituality and instead look inside yourself to find the in*spir*ation and enjoyment that your spiritual nature provides.

When I tell people that they are spiritual beings who are trying to be human, they often look at me in disbelief. But then I ask them to think about the energy that surrounds a newborn child. All those who have seen a new baby always agree that, yes, they truly do come 'trailing clouds of glory'; you can feel and almost see the divine spark within them. Then of course all we need to do is remember that we too arrived like this, exuding our own glorious and harmonious spiritual energy. As we grew up and became more preoccupied with 'doing' rather than simply 'being' we began to lose touch with our spiritual roots, but we can easily find them again. Our spiritual journey does not require that we travel into unfamiliar territory; we have been here before when we were very young and we just need to reconnect with that experience.

EXERCISE:

When you were a child
(A)

- Find some photos of you when you were a babe in arms. Look closely and lovingly at that gorgeous child; you were perfect, you *are still perfect.*
- Now look at yourself as a toddler and then as you started school. What a sweet girl you were. What a sweet girl you *are.*

- Pin up some of these photos where you can see them every day and let yourself love this child within you.

I have a photo of my mother, my daughter, my granddaughter and myself as toddlers. There we sit in the same frame looking utterly cute; butter wouldn't melt in our mouths! Sometimes it does me good to look at myself in the same way that I look at my granddaughter: without judgements and with complete adoration. Spend time with these photos of yourself and try talking to relatives about your childhood. If your parents are alive get them to tell you about some of your early exploits. The more you do this the more likely you are to resurrect some early memories. Ah, that gorgeous little girl hasn't gone anywhere, she is still a part of you and she wants some FUN!

(B)

- List some fun activities that you enjoyed when you were young. Now get out and do some of them. If you haven't got children try taking a niece or nephew to the park and get on a swing yourself. Try the roundabout; that dizzy feeling might bring back the distant past. Go to the fair and eat candyfloss, go ice-skating, ride a donkey on the beach. . .

Get in touch with the fun-loving girl that you are and you will be amazed by the change in your energy. Welcome joy, enthusiasm and fun into your life and your inner world will blossom. Learn to 'be' and you will relax and feel such a great sense of inner satisfaction and delight.

(C)

- Find some crayons (doesn't the smell of them take you back?) and some paper and draw a picture of yourself as a child. Use the hand that you don't usually use. Try drawing yourself with your parents and maybe the house where you lived.

Keep the girl in you alive and buzzing; she will give you so much joy.

We are all connected

As you tune into your spiritual awareness you will begin to sense a wonderful feeling of connection with the energy of the universe. Feelings of separation and isolation will fall away as you experience being a part of something so much larger than yourself. I once heard someone explain the illusion of our separateness from each other by comparing us to trees.

All trees appear to stand alone, although their leaves may whisper to each other and their branches may touch in the gentle breezes. But despite the fact that all trees appear to be separate, deep in the earth their roots are often intertwined with each other. And the earth unites them all. What a beautiful image this is!

Sit quietly and contemplate this image. If you can go outside and see real trees then all the better. Look at these trees (real or imagined) and see the way they stand so proud and upward reaching and seemingly so alone. Now become aware of their strong roots, which depend upon the earth for their nourishment. Visualise the interlocking root systems beneath the soil. As your trees rustle in the breeze, recognise that although they stand alone they are deeply connected. In just such a way we too are united in the material/spiritual universe. You are not alone; we are all connected. Think about this image as you go about your daily affairs.

Confident brain waves

When you engage with your spiritual energy you actually change the frequency of your brain waves.

Imagine the sound of the ocean as its waves pound continually and rhythmically against the shore. All things have a pulse and rhythm just like the sea: sound and light form waves and each sound we hear and colour we see has its unique frequency and vibration. Your body works as a rhythmic, pulsating organism and your brain makes waves that change according to your state. Brain activity increases when we are stressed and this heightened frequency makes us feel even worse (you know only too well what this is like). Every single thought you have affects the rhythm of your brain waves and your daily pressures just increase the frequencies. But when you are asleep your brain engages in a different level of awareness, the alpha level. Here the frequency is lower and you are relaxed and at ease.

Scriptwriter, author and poet Julia Cameron has something interesting to say about the alpha state: 'Walks are the generators for me of what I call my "alpha ideas". These alpha ideas are the ideas that seem to come from a higher source than myself, suggesting better solutions to my creative or daily problems than my ordinary thinking does.'

Yes, if we can change the frequency of our brain waves

from beta to alpha and still remain awake and conscious then we can tap into a more creative and expansive source of energy. I don't know about you but I often find that my 'ordinary thinking' (at beta level) can leave me with little inspiration and creativity. When I am writing a book I often take time out to get on the alpha frequency and buzz up my energy. Whilst Julia Cameron likes to put on her walking shoes I like to go to the gym or have a swim or dig the garden. Any repeated physical activities can change your consciousness by switching off your logical left brain activity (beta level) and engaging the creative and inspired energy of your right brain (alpha level).

In the lower frequency alpha state we are centred, confident, calmer and clearer. But we don't have to pound the pavement or brave the gym to change our state of mind. We can simply get into this condition by relaxing, slowing down our breathing, visualising, meditating or taking part in activities like yoga or t'ai chi. Any of the 'Inner Reflections' in this book will take you from beta to alpha.

Begin to notice the difference in yourself when you are at alpha or beta frequency. If you are feeling low in confidence and uninspired then you need to slow down your brain frequency. Do this now by stopping and relaxing and consciously slowing down your breathing. Did you know that when you take slower and more even breaths others pick up on this immediately and perceive you as being confident and self-assured?

INSTANT BOOST

THINGS TO DO LATER

WHENEVER YOU ARE RUSHING ABOUT TRYING TO DO EVERYTHING OR BE EVERYTHING OR HAVE EVERYTHING YOU WILL FEEL MUCH LESS THAN YOUR CONFIDENT BEST AND YOU WILL DEFINITELY BE IN BETA MODE. WHEN YOU NEXT FEEL LIKE THIS TAKE IMMEDIATE ACTION.

- STOP 'DOING' AND SIT DOWN WITH A PENCIL AND PAPER. YES, YOU HAVE GOT TIME TO DO THIS!
- WRITE A LIST OF ALL THE THINGS THAT ARE GOING ROUND AND ROUND IN YOUR HEAD. THESE WILL BE THINGS THAT YOU FEEL YOU 'SHOULD' OR 'MUST' DO.
- NOW CREATE A NEW LIST CALLED *THINGS I WILL DO LATER*. PIN IT UP ON THE WALL SO THAT YOU CAN REFER TO IT, *LATER*.
- IN THE MEANTIME JUST CONCENTRATE ON THE IMMEDIATE TASK IN HAND. STOP REMINDING YOURSELF ABOUT EVERYTHING ELSE, YOU DON'T NEED TO DO THAT ANY MORE BECAUSE YOU HAVE MADE YOUR LIST.
- ONCE YOU HAVE FINISHED ONE TASK YOU CAN THEN REFER TO YOUR LIST AND TAKE THE NEXT ITEM THAT NEEDS DOING.
- ACKNOWLEDGE THAT YOU ARE PROBABLY NOT GOING TO DO EVERYTHING TODAY SO WHY NOT RELEGATE SOME OF THE ITEMS ON YOUR LIST FOR LATER IN THE WEEK? THERE IS SOMETHING SO RESTFUL ABOUT CREATING A LIST OF THINGS TO DO LATER TODAY OR LATER THIS WEEK OR EVEN *VERY MUCH LATER*.

> IF YOU ARE A BIT OF A BUSY BEE JUST REMIND YOURSELF
> THAT WHEN YOUR ENERGY IS BALANCED YOU ARE GOING
> WITH THE FLOW. GIVE YOURSELF A BREAK AND INDULGE IN
> SOME WONDERFUL, RESTFUL, STRESS-FREE ALPHA WAVE
> ACTIVITY. YOU DESERVE IT!

Looking at the bigger picture

When negativity strikes and we lose confidence we become so much 'smaller'. Suddenly it can seem that we have lost our power and have become totally insignificant in the grand scheme of things. I think that we do actually look physically smaller when our energy is depressed; we withdraw into ourselves with our heads down and our body language shrieks of low self-worth. When we feel like this we are inclined to focus on problematic details and we are apt to lose any sense of perspective. It's at times like these that we most need to lighten our energy. One simple way to do this is to start to recognise the synchronistic events in your life.

The eminent psychologist Carl Jung said: 'Synchronicity suggests that there is an interconnection or unity of causally unrelated events.' Take a moment to reflect on this. How do you respond when life presents you with a remarkable set of previously unconnected circumstances that demonstrates that everything is just coming together? Perhaps you can't remember when this last happened or maybe you just believe in 'coincidences'. But when we look at the bigger picture of our lives we can usually see undeniable evidence of the impeccable timing and synchronicity that give a sense of meaning and purpose to our days.

Try this now: Take any area of your life and work

backwards from where you are now in order to see 'how it all began'. How did you find your present home? How did you meet your partner? What were the circumstances surrounding you getting your current job? Can you see how and *why* one thing led to another?

Caroline's story

Caroline, 44, is a library assistant who is married and has two grown-up children. When her youngest left for university Caroline fell into a very negative state where nothing felt meaningful to her any more and she just couldn't be bothered with anything. A friend bought her a month's life coaching with me and at our first conversation she registered her doubts that anything could be done for her. She said that she felt that 'the magic has gone from my life; nothing seems to matter and I have lost my oomph'. This sort of emptiness points towards a spiritual imbalance. We all need to know that there is a point to what goes on in our daily life and when we can't make that important connection life gets boring, dreary and meaningless.

I introduced Caroline to the notion of synchronicity and the way that it works. I asked her to start to look for evidence of synchronicity in her life. This meant becoming aware of connections, patterns and meanings in everything that happened each day. At first she was sceptical and didn't really understand what she was doing, but this soon changed. I asked her to keep a synchronicity diary for a week and this is what happened.

On the first day she woke up thinking of a friend and then met her in the street some hours later. She said that she thought that this was 'just a coincidence'. In the afternoon at work she heard someone mention an administrative job vacancy at the theatre in the town and when she got home her husband had left a message on the answer machine telling her that he had heard about a great job that she might be interested in at the theatre. Caroline had been an amateur dramatics enthusiast before she had her children but had seemed to lose all interest in the theatre since. She said that she was amazed that her husband had thought she might be interested and that it was 'most peculiar' that she had heard about the job too. Caroline felt that it was 'one coincidence too many' and she said that she 'had a feeling' that she must follow it up.

From this point on Caroline seemed to move on to a different level of awareness. She started to talk about 'hunches' and 'gut feelings' and she said that suddenly everything had got 'more interesting'. It's true that as soon as you begin to concentrate on synchronicity your life takes on a new dimension, and as your inner awareness develops you begin to attract even more meaningful events.

Caroline followed up the vacancy but decided that it wasn't for her. But she *did* decide that she wanted to get back into acting and so she joined a local drama group. In one week Caroline had shifted her energy from low and depressed to high and interested and all it took was a change of focus.

As soon as you begin to recognise the synchronicity at work in your life you open a door to greater spiritual awareness. Wake up to the meaning behind the signs, coincidences, flashes of insight and intuition, hunches and dreams that fill your life. Let your spiritual energy revitalise you and remind you that you are going with the flow.

Listen to your intuition

The more you listen to your intuition the more powerful it becomes.

- Think of a time when you acted on a hunch and things turned out well. And what about that time when you 'knew' that you should do something but you didn't follow your 'gut' reaction and things went wrong?
- Now fast forward to the present moment and ask yourself what your intuition is telling you at the moment. These might be quite small things like: read that book; take some exercise; phone a friend; book a mini break; improve your diet. Or maybe it's pointing out some much more important issues: finish that relationship; look for a new job; stop smoking.
- Make a note of all your answers and ask yourself if you have acted on your inner guidance; if not, then why haven't you? You can be sure that if your intuition is sending strong messages that you are disregarding, then you will be feeling stuck, negative and low in confidence.

Begin to listen to your gut feelings and hunches and honour them. Trust your inner knowing and follow its guidance and your energy will be uplifted.

And be happy just to be here

When you cultivate a deep appreciation of, and love for, life you open the door to your spirituality and everything will start to click into place. If this feels very hard for you to do right now, take inspiration from the following story.

Jane Tomlinson, 40, is a British cancer sufferer who has broken a world record to become the first terminally ill person to complete the full Ironman triathlon in Florida.

The seventeen-hour challenge involved swimming two miles, completing a 112-mile bike ride and running a full marathon. Jane has already cycled from Rome to Leeds, completed three London marathons, three London triathlons and two half-Ironman triathlons to raise money for cancer charities. She said that the Florida event would be her last challenge.

Her husband Mike, 43, said that people shouldn't assume that Jane found the events easy. He said: 'Jane's dying an awfully painful death. Don't be misled by thinking that because she does endurance events she doesn't suffer. The training and races put a huge strain on her body constantly, leaving her in agony. Yet she still has to get to work daily and take annual leave to do the events.'

Jane is a sublime example of the power of focused, go-getting energy. And after all that she has gone through, and all that she is going through she had this to say: 'I am happy just to be here.'

Try this affirmation throughout the day. Say to yourself:

I am happy just to be here

When you go with the flow you take what life offers you and make the very most of it. Take life and grab it and go for it and love it – there is absolutely nothing else you need to do.

20 Easy ways to get into the flow

1 Get passionate about your life.

2 Stop rushing around and take time to stand and stare.

3 Reflect on the differences you make to those around you.

4 Count your blessings every day.

5 Think positively.

6 Take time out to 'be' rather than to 'do'.

7 Stay in touch with your emotions.

8 Act assertively.

9 Enjoy a playful activity.

10 Slow down your breathing.

11 Appreciate the small things in life.

12 Love your goals.

13 Tap into your intuition and act upon it.

14 Have some fun!

15 Remember that we are all connected; you are never alone.

16 Get into the alpha state and relax!

17 Become aware of the synchronicity in your life.

18 Look for the bigger picture.

19 Be happy just to be here.

20 Tell someone how much you love them.

INNER REFLECTION

RELAX

SIT COMFORTABLY, CLOSE YOUR EYES AND BECOME CONSCIOUS OF YOUR BREATHING.

YOUR MIND WILL AUTOMATICALLY FILL WITH MANY THOUGHTS. TRY NOT TO FOLLOW THEM OR THEY WILL DISTRACT YOU. BECAUSE YOUR MIND NEVER STOPS, YOUR THOUGHTS WILL KEEP COMING SO JUST NOTICE THEM AND THEN LET THEM GO.

EACH TIME YOU GET DISTRACTED JUST COME BACK TO YOUR BREATHING. FOLLOW YOUR IN BREATHS AND OUT BREATHS: IN AND OUT, IN AND OUT, AND AS YOU DO SO START TO BECOME AWARE OF YOUR BODY.

NOW IMAGINE THAT YOUR WHOLE BODY IS RELAXING. BEGIN WITH YOUR TOES AND FEEL A GREAT WAVE OF RELAXATION SWEEPING THROUGH YOUR FEET, CALVES AND THIGHS. YOU CAN FEEL YOUR LEGS GETTING HEAVIER AND HEAVIER. LET THIS CALM AND RELAXED FEELING TRAVEL UP INTO YOUR LOWER BACK AND ABDOMEN. FEEL THE WARM PEACEFUL ENERGY MOVE INTO YOUR CHEST, UPPER BACK AND SHOULDERS. AS YOU LET YOUR SHOULDERS DROOP YOUR BODY IS VERY HEAVY, WARM, RELAXED AND PEACEFUL.

NOW LET GO OF ALL TENSION IN YOUR HANDS, ARMS, NECK, HEAD AND FACE. AS YOU FEEL YOUR FACIAL MUSCLES LETTING GO YOUR JAWS AND EYES FEEL HEAVY AND RELAXED.

YOU ARE NOW COMPLETELY COMFORTABLE AND AT EASE AND A WONDERFUL FEELING OF INNER PEACE AND SERENITY SURROUNDS YOU. ENJOY!

WHEN YOU ARE READY COME BACK SLOWLY INTO THE ROOM. THIS IS A GREAT ROUTINE FOR ANY TIME WHEN YOU NEED TO LET GO OF THE STRESSES AND STRAINS OF THE DAY AS YOU TAP INTO YOUR SPIRITUAL AWARENESS.

Change Your Life

There are costs and risks to a programme of action, but they are far less than the long-range risks and costs of comfortable inaction.

Finding the confidence to change

Low self-confidence creates a feeling that 'nothing I do will ever work', and I find that the people who are most insecure are the ones who are most cynical and disparaging about the possibilities for self-change. If we lose belief in ourselves we lose the power to dream and then life becomes dull and hopeless.

So what are we to do when we are down and out and need to make changes but can't drum up the energy and confidence that self-change requires? The answer lies in an approach that addresses two important issues: that we recognise and understand the stages and process of self-change and that we increase our personal levels of self-awareness. If we can't find the inner confidence to improve our lives at all levels then we need to investigate our personal doubts and fears. Knowledge is power and the more we know about how we tick the more likely we are to be able to turn things around and rejuvenate our lives. Change comes whether we like it or not and on a buoyant day we find it much easier to ride those breaking waves and go with the flow. But on a day when our energy is lower we might be intimidated and overwhelmed by those same new challenges.

Jenny's and Sarah's story
Jenny and Sarah recently lost their jobs at a local radio station. Jenny took the chance to take more training and then started sending out résumés to radio and TV networks all over the UK. A few months later she landed a plum job at the BBC. Jenny describes her redundancy as 'the best thing that could have happened to her'. Sarah was devastated to lose her job and became angry and depressed and is now on medication and is still unemployed. She says that losing her job has made her ill and that she is 'too down to do anything about finding more work'. Both girls are young and equally talented and of course Sarah might well ride this storm and pick up the pieces when she is feeling better. But notice the different responses they showed to change.

Adapting to change

Change can be exhilarating, like a breath of fresh air blowing through our lives. When change feels exciting it is because we think we can deal with it; it doesn't challenge us too much and the outcome is one we would like. You might have experienced this at the start of a new intimate relationship when the newness of it all changed your life in a magical way so that nothing seemed the same any more and you felt like you were walking on air. Think of a time when you were

INSTANT BOOST

YOUR CHANGING YEAR

CONSIDER HOW THE PROCESS OF CHANGE HAS AFFECTED YOU OVER THE PAST YEAR. THERE WILL BE SOME ASPECTS THAT YOU WELCOMED AND OTHERS THAT WERE MORE DIFFICULT AND THERE WILL HAVE BEEN SMALL CHANGES AND BIG ONES. WHATEVER YOUR YEAR HAS BEEN LIKE YOU HAVE SURVIVED AND FACED THE CHALLENGES THAT CHANGES ALWAYS BRING.

NOW THINK OF TEN CHANGES THAT MADE DEMANDS ON YOU THIS YEAR.

1 ....
2 ....
3 ....
4 ....
5 ....
6 ....
7 ....
8 ....
9 ....
10 ....

TAKE EACH ONE AND THINK OF THE PROCESS THAT YOU WENT THROUGH AS YOU DEALT WITH EACH NEW OCCURRENCE.

BECOME AWARE OF THE WAYS YOU DEAL WITH THE UNEXPECTED. ARE YOU THROWN BY THE NEW OR ARE YOU MORE SANGUINE AND ADAPTABLE? DID SOME CHANGES HAVE

A BIGGER PERSONAL IMPACT THAN OTHERS? IF SO WHY DO
YOU THINK THIS IS? ON REFLECTION, DO YOU THINK THAT
THERE ARE ANY WAYS THAT YOU COULD HAVE REACTED THAT
WOULD HAVE MADE THINGS EASIER FOR YOU? AND WITH THE
BENEFIT OF HINDSIGHT, DID ANY OF THESE CHANGES BRING
A BENEFIT THAT YOU COULDN'T SEE AT THE TIME?

LOOK AT THE CHANGES THAT YOU ARE GOING THROUGH
RIGHT NOW; HOW CAN YOU BEST ACCOMMODATE THEM?
REMEMBER THAT YOU ARE AN ADAPTABLE AND FLEXIBLE
SURVIVOR OR YOU WOULD NEVER BE READING THIS BOOK.

delighted by the prospect of change. Your thoughts, feelings
and behaviour at this time would have reflected your
confidence and self-belief; you *knew* you could cope, you
felt in control and you were energised and motivated.

But change can feel threatening and frightening, like the
mat is being pulled from under our feet and we don't know
what will happen next; this sort of change often feels totally
unexpected and challenging. I'm sure you can think of a
situation where you were dragged kicking and screaming out
of your comfort zone. Just cast your mind back to your
thoughts and feelings when this last happened to you. And
how did you behave *in extremis*? When fears and doubts fill
our mind we find it hard to mobilise our energy and go with
the flow. Our low confidence levels can leave us feeling out
of control and unable to cope and this can only lead into a
negative cycle where things feel even more out of control.
But we can always take charge of a situation by rising to the
occasion and drawing on our inner resources. We need only
change our thoughts, feelings or behaviour to create a new
scenario where we can feel relaxed and in charge.

Your thoughts, feelings and behaviour are always changing. Your confidence levels can alter from one moment to the next. You might be swinging along full of positive self-beliefs, feeling great and then . . . something happens. This 'something' can be anything that knocks you off balance and changes your mood by making you question your beliefs. And suddenly, the thoughts that were supporting your self-confidence change and you sink into a whirlpool of negative self-beliefs. Instead of believing that you deserve the best and that you can 'make things happen', you are now believing that you are worthless and powerless to change anything – you have become a victim of circumstances! The speed at which this change can happen is really quite frightening and as soon as the quality of your thoughts changes, your feelings and behaviour correspond. The good news is that once you know how this process works you can intervene as soon as you begin to feel self-criticism and self-doubt kicking in.

E X E R C I S E :

When high confidence changes to low confidence

Think of a time when you felt full of confidence and then something occurred that totally demoralised you. Perhaps someone criticised you in a particularly sensitive area, or maybe you felt shown up in some way or possibly you were intimidated by changing circumstances and felt out of your depth.

1   Describe your thoughts about yourself when you were feeling confident, *before* the event occurred.
2   How did you feel at this time?

3 How did you act, before the event?

Now, try to reconstruct the exact circumstances surrounding this situation. Recreate the sensations that were linked with losing your confidence.

4 What were your thoughts about yourself *after* the event?
5 What feelings do you associate with your loss of confidence at this time?
6 How did your behaviour change after the event occurred?

Reflect on your answers. We'll be coming back to them in the next exercise.

This process of losing and regaining our confidence is a never-ending piece of work. People often ask me how they can stay confident all of the time and of course this is impossible. Although we can learn to be confident and optimistic, we can never stay unaffected by the ups and downs of life. We will always be challenged by something or other because our lives are always changing and moving on. Accept this! Accept that you will be challenged but remember that you have all the resilience, stamina and grit that you will ever need to deal with whatever life throws at you: let this give you confidence. Next time you are knocked off your confident perch just remember that you can pick yourself up, dust yourself down and get back up there.

INSTANT BOOST

FAKE IT UNTIL YOU MAKE IT

YOU HAVE PROBABLY HEARD THIS OFTEN-QUOTED LIFE COACHING MAXIM. CLIENTS ARE SOMETIMES CONCERNED THAT IT MEANS PRETENDING TO BE SOMETHING YOU ARE NOT AND SO SOMEHOW BEING UNTRUE TO YOURSELF.

DON'T BE CONCERNED; WHEN WE SAY 'FAKE IT UNTIL YOU MAKE IT' WE ARE JUST TALKING ABOUT STEPPING INTO YOUR CONFIDENT SHOES (EVEN WHEN YOU DON'T FEEL CONFIDENT).

THE MOST OBVIOUS EXAMPLE OF THIS IS ADOPTING ASSERTIVE BODY LANGUAGE IN ORDER TO GIVE THE APPEARANCE OF CALM AND SELF-ASSURANCE. WHEN YOU HOLD YOU HEAD HIGH, SMILE AND WALK WITH EASE YOU WILL LOOK AND YOU WILL FEEL CONFIDENT. OTHERS WILL RESPOND TO YOUR CHARISMA AND PERCEIVE YOU AS A CONFIDENT PERSON, WHICH GIVES YOU MORE CONFIDENCE SO THAT BEFORE YOU KNOW IT YOU HAVE STOPPED FAKING IT AND YOU HAVE BECOME IT.

ACT CONFIDENTLY AND YOU WILL FIND YOURSELF FEELING CONFIDENT AND THINKING WELL OF YOURSELF.

WHEN YOUR CONFIDENCE IS SHATTERED GET OUT YOUR HEELS, PUT ON SOME GLITZ AND GLOSS, TAKE A DEEP BREATH, SMILE AND STEP OUT THERE AND JUST FAKE IT.

VERY SOON YOU WILL BE FEELING FABULOUS, BECAUSE YOU ARE FABULOUS!

The cycle of change

Review your answers to the previous exercise. Notice the particular relationship between your thoughts, feelings and behaviour before and after the situation that swept you from feeling confident to lacking confidence. It is possible to change the effects of this process – you can retrieve your self-confidence. The diagram called 'The cycle of change' on the next page shows how you can do this.

Take your answers to questions 4, 5 and 6 and insert them in the appropriate places in diagram (A). Describe the demoralising event in the space provided. Now look at your completed diagram (A).

What does it show you about the relationship between your thoughts, feelings and behaviour? Do these elements have a knock-on effect? Do they seem to create each other?

Look at the answers you have inserted in the diagram. Which, if any, of those reactions could you change?

Could you change your thoughts about the situation? For example, would you have been so crushed if you had been able to maintain a strong belief in yourself, regardless of the circumstances?

Could you change your feelings surrounding the event? For example, would it have been possible to bring some humour into the situation to lighten the load?

Would it be possible to act differently? Perhaps you didn't say what you would have liked to have said or maybe you said too much.

Reflect on the event, thoughts, feelings and actions that cost you your self-confidence. There is always so much scope for us to

A

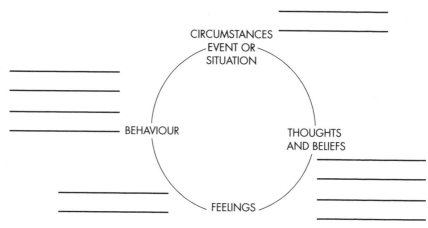

CIRCUMSTANCES
EVENT OR
SITUATION

BEHAVIOUR

THOUGHTS
AND BELIEFS

FEELINGS

B

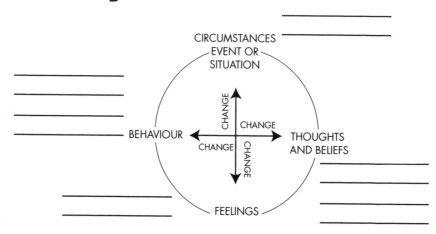

CIRCUMSTANCES
EVENT OR
SITUATION

BEHAVIOUR

THOUGHTS
AND BELIEFS

CHANGE

CHANGE

CHANGE

CHANGE

FEELINGS

THE CYCLE OF CHANGE

change, unless we prefer to stay stuck for some reason. The change cycle is a useful tool for helping to understand our reactions to circumstances and to see how we could cope differently and maintain our confidence levels.

Think of one reaction that you could change. Insert this in the appropriate place in diagram (B). How does this change the other elements in diagram (B)?

Now you have changed one response in the diagram, fill in the other spaces. Has everything changed? Has this response changed your perception of the initial circumstances? Be as creative as you can. Feel free to use your imagination to create a new take on this scenario. If a similar situation occurred again do you think that you could maintain your confidence levels?

Draw your own change cycles and use them when you are looking low self-confidence in the eye. Be creative: remember that you can always change. If your reactions can create low self-confidence then they can also create high self-confidence. Always choose reactions that support high confidence and self-belief.

Change yourself

The desire to change most often follows a spate of discontent and disenchantment. But don't ever let these feelings undermine you; see them as a reflection of your need to get up and go and *change something*.

Florence Nightingale recognised the meaning of this when she said: '(If) there were none who were discontented with what they have, the world would never reach for anything better.' So whenever you find yourself feeling fed-up and stuck remember that this only means that you *are ready to move on* and reach for new goals. And this becomes quite easy to do once we start to look closely at our own thoughts, feelings and behaviour.

Looking back at Jenny and Sarah, we can see how their differing attitudes affected their outcomes. Jenny had the confidence to overcome and indeed make the best of what she could have regarded as a negative situation. She let her positive self-belief energise the process of change and create new possibilities. Sarah's lack of self-confidence just drained her energy as she fell into a negative trap of despair and inaction.

You can always move from the negative cycle of defeat to the positive cycle of success, you just need to discover where your energy is blocked. You know only too well how damaging a self-critical thought can be as it creates a negative chain reaction that affects you at all levels, influencing your feelings and actions. Positive change happens when you:

Change your thoughts
Change your feelings
Change your actions

Let's look at each of these in turn.

Change your thoughts
If you are believing the worst about yourself then these negative thoughts need to change. One of the most powerful ways to alter negative beliefs is to use positive affirmations (sometimes called mantras). So, instead of thinking that you are *useless, no good, always make mistakes, can never be successful* . . . etc. you contradict and replace these negatives with their exact opposites.

Make a list of any of your thoughts, ideas or beliefs that might be hindering your progress and stopping you realising your goals. Now take this list of negative affirmations and turn them around. The following example shows how you can do this.

Negative affirmation	change to	Positive affirmation
I am a loser	➤	I am a winner
I am not clever enough	➤	I am clever enough
I am a victim	➤	I am in control
I can never fit in	➤	I am good enough
I am a failure	➤	I am a success
I can't change	➤	I can change

Be sure to keep your affirmations positive and in the present tense (if you affirm that you 'will be' something, it will always stay there, in the future). Concentrate on what you want more of rather than what you want less of (what you put your attention on grows). So, rather than saying, 'I want to be less negative', you would say, 'I *am* positive'. Make it real and feel the change happen in the moment that you say it.

Positive affirmations often get a bad press. I was on a TV programme recently where someone was laughing at the possibility that repeating the phrase 'I am fabulous' could ever actually make us fabulous. But he was missing the point: we are what we believe we are and we fulfil our expectations of ourself. If we *truly believed* that we were fabulous then we would create the ideas, feelings and actions that would support our great self-image. I am a big fan of affirmations. I say them and sing them and I have them written on cards on my desk, in my handbags, briefcase, pocket . . . You name it I have them there! I surround myself with positive consciousness. Even life coaches need to be reminded to keep upbeat.

When I wrote my first book I didn't have a contract, I was just writing in the hope that a publisher would be interested in it when it was finished. In the process of writing I used all the techniques that I am talking about here because I needed to keep confident in order to keep going. When I got stuck or lost my nerve I would put affirmations on to the page I was writing, typing things like, *I am a successful author, I am a good writer, this book is excellent. . .*etc. I would keep typing these affirmations until I had pushed up my energy and my confidence levels enough to begin writing again. Then I would delete them and carry on with my chapter. This technique saw me through some rough patches and eventually before the book was finished I just knew and expected that my manuscript would be published. Believe me, affirmations work; you just have to keep at them.

Change your feelings

The techniques I used to change my manuscript into a real book on the shelf included visualisations as well as affirmations. If they are to work, positive affirmations must be supported by positive visions. Together they create an upsurge of positive emotions, including high expectations and feelings of confidence and success.

Fourteen years ago when I was writing that first book we were living in Gorran Haven in Cornwall. We were twelve miles away from the nearest town, St Austell. On a Saturday the whole family would go to town and the children would have swimming lessons and then we would all go to WH Smiths. This branch is very small and doesn't stock a lot of books but every Saturday my husband and I and the three children would undergo a ceremony in front of the lifestyle shelf (the nearest genre to self-help at the time). We would all imagine my book facing outward on the shelf. By then I had a title so we all had a real image to focus on. This went on for the whole of the two years that I was writing that book. And then, by the time it was finished I was in absolutely no doubt that it would be a great success; I had already 'seen' it on the shelf so many times and so of course I knew it would get there! I am confident that it was the techniques that helped pull me and my manuscript through to a great outcome.

Creative visualisation is a brilliant technique to use whenever you are working towards a new goal. Use the affirmations that you need and then visualise your dream coming true. The pictures in your mind as well as the thoughts you carry help to create your reality. When your thoughts and images are positive and achieving then you will have every chance of success.

Get into a relaxed state and *see, feel* and *experience* yourself enacting your dreams. If you want to be more successful, see yourself thriving and hear the admiration of others. Be specific and fill in all the details (what will your success look like, how will it feel?). Really experience your success in full Technicolor; *feel* what it is like to be the person you would most like to be. Let your positive visualisations replace all those old pictures of yourself that didn't work for you.

NEGATIVE AFFIRMATIONS	+	NEGATIVE VISUALISATIONS	→	OLD NEGATIVE REALITIES
POSITIVE AFFIRMATIONS	+	POSITIVE VISUALISATIONS	→	NEW CHANGED REALITIES

Change your actions

New positive affirmations and visualisations, fired with the enthusiasm of total commitment, will generate the action you will need to create a new outcome. Action never stands alone because our behaviour patterns are a reflection of the ways we think and feel about our world and ourselves.

There are two ways to behave: we can choose to be consciously creative or we can act like a victim. If you see yourself as a victim then you will never get a meaningful grip on your life. Decisions will not be carried to a conclusion; you will always be someone else's doormat; something will always stop you from reaching your goal and this will always be someone else's fault. If this sounds like you then just decide to break this negative pattern now! Creative behaviour requires an open-hearted, trusting and questing approach and comes from a sense of personal responsibility; there is no one to blame, you create your own life circumstances, the ball is always in your court; hit it!

Victim consciousness changes to creative consciousness as soon as you change the way you act, and start to behave assertively. It's not what you do, it's the way that you do it that counts, so get out of blaming mode and into assertive mode right now.

10 Ways to be assertive

1 Respect yourself and others.
2 Know what you want.
3 Take full responsibility for your actions.
4 Use good clear communication skills.
5 Be ready to take a risk.
6 Trust that the universe will support you.

7 Keep things in perspective.
8 Be flexible but stand your ground on major issues.
9 Express your true feelings (this includes saying no).
10 Smile and go with the flow.

INSTANT BOOST

10 THINGS I WANT TO DO

IF YOU ARE FEELING STUCK BUT YOU DON'T QUITE KNOW WHAT TO DO TO GET OUT OF YOUR RUT, TRY THIS TECHNIQUE.

THINK OF TEN THINGS THAT YOU WOULD LOVE TO DO. CHOOSE SOME SHORT-TERM AND SOME LONGER-TERM GOALS. FOR EXAMPLE: JOIN A GYM; HAVE A FACIAL; VISIT THE STATES; TRAIN TO BE A COUNSELLOR; STICK AT MY POSITIVE AFFIRMATIONS . . .

I WOULD LOVE TO:

1 ....
2 ....
3 ....
4 ....
5 ....
6 ....
7 ....
8 ....
9 ....
10 ....

> GO BACK OVER EACH GOAL AND CONSIDER WHAT IT WOULD TAKE TO SET EACH OF THESE GOALS IN MOTION. CHOOSE ONE OF THE SHORT-TERM GOALS AND TAKE THAT FIRST STEP. AS SOON AS YOU DO THIS YOU WILL CHANGE YOUR ENERGY FLOW AND THINGS WILL START TO MOVE AGAIN.
>
> YOU WILL BE MOST SURPRISED BY THE WAY THAT YOU FEEL ABOUT YOURSELF AS YOU MOVE FORWARD; YOU WILL BE MOTIVATED, ENERGISED, FOCUSED AND FILLED WITH CONFIDENCE. TRY IT AND SEE.

Get SMART about your goals

There is only one thing standing between you and your goals and that is you! If you really want to go for something then *absolutely nothing* will stand in your way. Throughout this book we have looked at so many ordinary people, just like you and me, who have had the confidence to reach for their dreams. We have seen how these people have overcome personal self-doubts and bounced back again and again when things have become difficult. Successful people like this have one important secret: *they know exactly want they want.* Now this might not sound very impressive, but in fact it is the most important element of success. You will never reach a dream unless you have named that dream. It's so easy to keep your innermost hopes and desires in fantasy land and to visit them every now and again. How many times have you heard people say things like: Oh I wish I could do that; be that; have that, as if these goals are mere wishes with no hope of coming true. But of course the only way to convert dreams into reality is to name your goal and be SMART about it.

Make your goal:

Specific: Clarify your goal; what *exactly* do you want?

Measurable: Quantify your goal in some way so that you can evaluate your progress.

Attractive: If you love your goal you will achieve it and if you don't you won't be able to sustain your motivation.

Realistic: You must know in your heart of hearts that you can achieve your goal. Don't set it too high or you will get discouraged. But don't set it too low either, because you need to stretch yourself.

Time-framed: Specify a time for you to achieve each step along the way.

Example

Let's see how this works in practice. Imagine that your intimate relationship is not as loving and close as it was. You have decided that your goal is *to have better communication with my partner*. By naming your goal you have made it **specific.** You will **measure** your progress by looking for signs from him that he is as keen as you to get the relationship back on track. You **love** him and want the relationship to work so you are highly motivated. This is a **realistic** goal because you have had a very close relationship with him for the six months before it started to cool off.

You will give it six weeks of your dedicated effort and if it hasn't worked by then you will have a serious rethink about whether this relationship is worth continuing.

E X E R C I S E :

An action plan for change

Look back in your journal to your answers to the Life Zone
checklist on page 122. If you were less than pleased and
positive about any area of your life then something needs to
change; if you scored less than 6 in any zone there is action to
be taken and you are ready to take it!

- Once you have recognised the need to move, decide to stop
  looking at the problem and begin to focus on the solution.
- By concentrating on the solution you will discover your goal.
  If this is still hard try asking yourself this simple question:
  What do I want to happen here?
- Break down your goals into bite-sized chunks and then it will
  become much more manageable. Identify the steps you need
  to take.
- Keep your confidence high with positive energy. Use
  positive affirmations and visualisations to keep your goal
  alive and then follow through with assertive action.
- Check that your goals are SMART.

Take all the skills that you have learned in this book and
apply them to your life. Deep down inside you know exactly
who you are and what you want; you know that you are
fabulous, amazing and good enough to go for all your dreams.
Step into those confident shoes and step out into the world
and make your mark. Don't forget to love yourself on the
difficult days, and there will be difficult days, have no doubt.
But you know how to rise to your challenges and shatter your
glass ceilings; and each time you do this you will increase

your confidence. So don't let anything hold you back as you reach for your best in all that you do. Watch your greatest dreams unfold and feel the total confidence that this brings. I know that you can do this and you know it too.

INNER REFLECTION

WAKE UP

WE OFTEN LIVE OUR LIVES AS IF IN A DREAM, THINKING REGRETFULLY OR NOSTALGICALLY ABOUT THE PAST AND THINKING WISHFULLY ABOUT THE FUTURE. BUT POSITIVE SELF-CHANGE CAN ONLY HAPPEN WHEN WE ARE TOTALLY AWARE AND AWAKE AND IN THE MOMENT. WE CAN ONLY BE OUR NATURALLY CONFIDENT SELVES WHEN WE ARE GOING WITH THE FLOW AND FEELING ALIVE TO 'WHAT IS' RATHER THAN 'WHAT WAS' OR 'WHAT CAN BE'.

NOW YOU HAVE FINISHED READING ALL THE IDEAS IN THIS BOOK I WANT YOU TO JUST RELAX AND PUT ALL YOUR THOUGHTS ASIDE. INSTEAD, CONCENTRATE ON YOUR BREATHING UNTIL YOU ARE FEELING CALM AND CENTRED.

- SEE YOURSELF RADIATING POSITIVE AND CHARISMATIC ENERGY.
- FEEL YOURSELF FULL OF CONFIDENCE AND WELLBEING.
- REFLECT UPON THIS IMAGE OF YOU LOOKING AND FEELING YOUR VERY BEST AND GET INTO THE SKIN OF THIS FABULOUSLY CONFIDENT WOMAN.

IMAGINE YOURSELF BEING ABLE TO BE THIS FULL OF

CONFIDENCE AND WELLBEING EACH TIME YOU STEP OUT INTO THE WORLD. YOU ARE TOTALLY ALERT AND AWAKE TO EACH MOMENT AND YOU CAN LOVE YOUR LIFE *JUST THE WAY THAT IT IS*. YOU ARE ACCEPTING AND FORGIVING AND YOU CAN EASILY LET GO OF ANYTHING THAT HOLDS YOU BACK.

WAKE UP TO THIS PRESENT MOMENT AND TO EVERY OTHER MOMENT OF YOUR PRECIOUS LIFE: LIVE IT AND LOVE IT AND SHINE WITH INNER CONFIDENCE; YOU ARE AMAZING.

Epilogue
The Best Day Ever!

Grandma, I just loved it today, it was the best day ever!

ALASKA PORTER

My granddaughter Alaska lives quite a long way from us so when she visits she always stays for a while and we do lots of exciting things together. We go to Crazy Kids, an indoor playground where we jump around on the mattresses and play on the equipment; we visit Marsh Farm and feed sheep and make animal masks; we blow up a mini bouncy castle in the garden and fall around it in hysterics; we catch a train to the seaside; we go to the cinema, and we dress up a lot of paper dolls and do all sorts of things with glue and glittery stars . . . you get the picture, we just have a great time.

Last time she came to stay and we had returned from a freezing cold day at Marsh Farm, Alaska threw herself across the sofa and said, 'Grandma, I just loved today, it was the best day ever!' A few days later on the phone she was telling me about her day at school and she said, 'Oh it was the best day ever!' No wonder I love having her to stay, this girl really knows how to have a good time. She gets excited before we do anything, so we have a 'looking forward to' period; then she is always busy 'loving it' while we are there (wherever we go) and then she reflects on the good time we had and it's always the 'best day ever'.

Today is the most important day of your life. In these twenty-four hours you have the chance to love every moment and to appreciate everything about your miraculous existence. Take each day and live it to the full. Let yourself enjoy each moment wholeheartedly, don't hold anything back. Be the best you can be and let your mind, body and spirit flow easily and gracefully and confidently. Remember that your contribution always counts, so make it good. And as you take your love and joyfulness into the world know that everyone you meet is touched and affected by your positive mood.

Your originality and your special flair mean you are a fabulous, glorious and amazing woman, so love the skin you are in and know your true worth. Confidence is contagious so spread your charismatic energy far and wide. Each time you reach your positive best you are an inspiration to everyone around you; so let your light shine.

And if you are not feeling high in self-esteem right now, treat yourself well. Be kind to yourself when you are less than your confident best because at these challenging times you are learning to stretch and grow and change, and sometimes this process is painful. Admire your survival instincts and marvel at your ability to rise to each and every challenge. You are creative, capable and inspired and you have all the inner resources you will ever need; so never doubt yourself.

Your goal is total confidence so step out and take your rightful place at the very centre of your own life. Be what you can be and have the best day ever, every day. Do what you can do and reach for the very highest within you and know that you have what it takes to sparkle with confidence and glow from within.

I am so lucky to have the chance to write about the subject that is dearest to my heart. After all, it was my own quest for confidence that led me to writing my first book and here I am fourteen years later *still* finding plenty to say. I have loved writing *Weekend Confidence Coach* and I hope you have enjoyed reading it. If you would like to get in touch with me or find out more about my life-coaching services just go to www.weekendlifecoach.com or email me at lyndafield@weekendlifecoach.com

I look forward to hearing from you.

With all my best wishes

Lynda

References and Inspirational Books

Boldt, Laurence G, *Zen and the Art of Making a Living,*
   Arkana, 1999

Cameron, Julia, *The Vein of Gold,* Pan Books, 1997

Coelho, Paulo, *The Alchemist,* HarperCollins, 1999

Field, Lynda, *Creating Self-Esteem,* Vermilion, 2001
   The Self-Esteem Workbook, Vermilion, 2001
   Just Do it Now!, Vermilion, 2001
   365 Inspirations for a Great Life, Vermilion, 2002
   Be Yourself, Vermilion, 2003
   Weekend Life Coach, Vermilion, 2004

Hanh, Thich Nhat, *The Miracle of Mindfulness,* Rider, 1991
   Peace is Every Step, Rider, 1995

Hay, Louise, *Yon Can Heal Your Life,* Eden Grove Editions,
   1988

Juska, Jane, *A Round-heeled Woman,* Chatto & Windus,
   2003

Redfield, James, *The Celestine Prophecy,* Bantam, 1994

Schaef, Anne Wilson, *Meditations for Women Who do too
   Much,* HarperCollins, 1996

Seligman, Martin, *Learned Optimism,* Pocket Books, 1998

Sherfield, Robert M, *The Everything Self-Esteem Book,*
   Adams Media, 2004

Index

McManus, Michelle 59
meditation 28, 176
Miller, Arthur 97

negative
    cycle 24-5, 204-5
    thinking 133-4, 167-9,
        193-4
Nightingale, Florence 209
'now', the 10, 18, 135

optimism 10, 40, 111, 155-76
Osbourne, Sharon 54

perfection 21, 26, 73-5, 76
persistence 100, 151
positive action 110-27, 171
Positive Psychology 156-7,
    158, 161-2

Ravn, Karen 3
realism 71, 162-3
regrets 134-5
relaxation 60-1, 87, 153-4,
    172-5, 198-9,213
resentment 135
'lightness' ix, 3, 16, 89
risk-taking 62, 65,71-3

scarcity consciousness 167-8
Schaef, Anne Wilson 73-4
Scott, Alex 95-7, 101
self-awareness 75,78, 99-100,
    106
self-belief 7, 16, 23, 38, 46-61,
    65, 81, 106-7, 137-8, 152-3
self-confidence 3,4-5, 21, 47,
    55,121-2, 137-8, 200

self-criticism 27, 42, 56,
    99-100, 150-1
self-doubt 16-17, 39-40, 41,
    56
self-esteem 14, 23, 68-9, 169
self-help books 36-7,62-3,160,
    212-13
self-image 32-4, 42, 48-52, 57,
    118, 211
self-promotion 138, 139
Seligman, Martin 156, 157
SMART 10, 216-18
Smith, Marcelle D'Argy 131
spirituality 10, 177-99
synchronicity 193-5

timing 103-4
Tomlinson, Jane 197
trust 22, 159-60, 214

unique selling point 50-1, 52,
    141-3

victim 8, 17, 103, 149-50,
    214
visualisation 44-5, 60-1, 80,
    88-9, 92-3, 104-5, 136,
    172-5, 189-90, 212-13

Walters, Julie 54
Wigmore, Barry 95
Winfrey, Oprah 25, 156
winners 46-7,62,66,95-109,
    136, 151
Woodall, Trinny 12-13
worldview 167-9
worth 6-7, 22, 29-31, 34-5,
    43-5, 54, 134, 140-1, 169